Driving Southern

Driving Southern

Life in Cars

Edited by
RALPH BLAND
and MICHAEL BRASWELL

RESOURCE *Publications* · Eugene, Oregon

DRIVING SOUTHERN
Life in Cars

Resource Publications
An Imprint of Wipf and Stock Publishers
199 W. 8th Ave., Suite 3
Eugene, OR 97401

www.wipfandstock.com

PAPERBACK ISBN: 978-1-6667-4682-2
HARDCOVER ISBN: 978-1-6667-4683-9
EBOOK ISBN: 978-1-6667-4684-6

VERSION NUMBER 062222

Contents

Preface | 7

Acknowledgments | 9

1 See the USA | 1
   Ralph Bland

2 Love at First Ride | 7
   Anthony Cavender

3 My Horseless Carriage | 12
   Tom Burton

4 Mabel's Driving Rules | 15
   Roberta T. Herrin

5 A View from the Tailgate of an El Camino | 19
   Scott Braswell

6 Viva the Vega and Other Cars I Loved | 24
   Don Harris

7 Mustang Sally | 30
   Michael Braswell

8 Hello, Goodbye | 35
   Ralph Bland

9 From Beatlemania to Wildfire on I-40 | 41
   Tom Nahay

10 The Car Makes the Man | 49
   Bob Dietz

11 My Foreign Affairs | 56
   Ralph Bland

12 Mopar Madness | 63
   Alan Longmire

13 Automobilitis | 70
   Dan Kyte

14 My First Car | 72
   Jerry Leger

15 A Jeep Named Willys | 76
   William Miller

16 The Heap | 79
   Matt Lawson

17 A Wild Maverick | 85
   Jeffrey Walker

18 Growing Up Buick | 89
   Pete Kilbourne

19 The Mercury Man | 94
   Robert Brassell

20 My Camaro Romance | 99
   Bob Roberson

21 Thunder Road and Beyond | 103
   Susan Braswell

22 Nice While It Lasted | 105
   Bob Wilson

23 Corvette Crazy | 110
   Steve Morrison

24 The VW Campmobile | 113
   Michael Braswell

25 My Cars | 116
   Bill Carpenter

26 God's Four Plus One | 121
   George Spain

Preface

FROM ADMIRING THE POWER of Clydesdales pulling a farm wagon or a beer truck for a Budweiser commercial, to observing the stunning beauty of thoroughbreds racing at the Kentucky Derby, horse power, speed, and aesthetics have always played a central role in our culture. Although they may have for the most part, been supplanted by ever bigger and more powerful trucks and faster, more exotic sports cars, in an essential way, they are still the original flame of it all.

This collection of essays and stories cover a broad range of personal reflections and memories. Corvettes and Thunderbirds are parked next to Studebakers, Volkswagen Beetles and in some cases, cars that may defy description or an automobile heritage of any kind. First cars, family cars, even dream cars purchased later in life in response to an unrequited or misspent youth, roam the highways and backroads within these pages. Often hilarious or at least, good for a chuckle, the stories are about growing up, although for some of us, where cars and trucks are concerned, we never quite do.

On occasion, the stories also reflect more poignant and bittersweet memories that we drive through our lives. A right turn here, a wrong turn there, or a sudden stop, compliments of a telephone pole or a broken relationship, are also reflected in these essays. Whatever the case, through the ups and downs of our lives, it feels good to get on the road again, curious to see what is waiting around the next curve.

Ralph Bland
Michael Braswell

Acknowledgments

WE WANT TO THANK Tony Cavender for his encouragement and input. Thanks also to our wives, Veronica and Susan for helping us through various stages of manuscript preparation. A very special thank you goes to Roberta Herrin for the time she spent making this a better book. Finally, we want to thank everyone who contributed a story about the role cars and trucks played in their lives.

Ralph Bland
Michael Braswell

1 See the USA

Ralph Bland

IN 1967, I HAD bagged groceries and swept floors and cleaned re-
strooms for a year already and still wasn't close to having enough
money to buy my first car. It was entirely possible I had even less
money than when I started working the year before. I seemed to
always be buying something to eat on my break or pitching in
money for gas when a bunch of friends and I rode around in the
evenings after work. Drinking illegally purchased beer and smok-
ing cigarettes cost money I should have been saving. Each time I
made headway in my quest to save, I would end up buying a new
shirt or pay for a movie if I was going out on a date. There was also
the purchase of the latest Beatles album to play on my sorry excuse
of the stereo in my room so I could sing them in my head while I
was loading groceries into backseats of cars at Kroger.

   I was in a hopeless situation, not even treading water financially speaking, when my Uncle Dick stepped up. A life-long bach-
elor and Greyhound bus driver who lived with my spinster aunt in
a small town outside of Nashville, he took pity on me and decided
to bestow his high school graduation gift a year early, endowing
me with three hundred dollars to go with the four I'd managed to
save so I could buy a car and have wheels of my own. He explained
to my mother that a young man turning seventeen needed to have
a few adventures. My mother didn't much like the idea, but my dad
semi-agreed in principle and even donated a hundred dollars of
his own toward car insurance, stipulating that from there on out, it

would be my responsibility to take care of the car, including repairs while staying legally insured. He surprised me further by taking me down to Nashville Electric where he worked and introducing me to one of his friends in the Accounting Department, a widow named Winona who had a 1962 Chevrolet Impala she wanted to sell. Because I was my daddy's son, she dropped the price she so I could afford it. She figured if I was anything like my daddy, I was a good fellow and deserved a break.

I'd never held that much money before. When I counted six hundred dollars into Miss Winona's hand, I felt like I was giving birth—that my whole world was about to change. She signed over the title and handed me a ring of keys, and I went out and got into my new car. I'd taken it for a test drive a little earlier, but this time it was different. This time it was all mine.

I washed and polished my Chevy that afternoon until I thought my arm was going to fall off. I drove around after supper on a full tank of gas, getting used to the steering wheel, the dashboard lights, the radio, and the low and high beams on the dark road. The next morning couldn't come fast enough. I drove to school and picked out a choice parking place among all the other students' cars, the bright fancy automobiles bought for them by their parents. None of them had worked for their rides the way I had. Maybe my 1962 Chevy wasn't as shiny and new with four-in-the-floor or bucket seats, but I was still proud of it. Parked in its prime spot, it said to the rest of the world that I had finally arrived and everybody might as well start getting used to it. For the first time in as long as I could remember, I felt like I was as good as anybody else. It was a feeling that had been a long time coming.

A grand moment was spent after school was dismissed that afternoon, when I walked to my gleaming 1962 Chevy Impala, unlocked the door and got inside, giving everyone in the parking lot the opportunity to see who this new car belonged to, who was the cool driver who'd recently entered into the elite social caste of automobile hierarchy. Even if my V-8 didn't pulsate and hit a lick like some of the expensive muscle cars the other kids drove, the sound was still music to my ears. I had a hard time deciding if I wanted to turn the radio on to a Top 40 station or leave it off and enjoy the low rumble of the Impala's engine.

I went home, changed clothes and grabbed a bite to eat before leaving for work. My shift at Kroger always lasted until thirty minutes past closing time at nine, which meant mealtime for me was a fifteen-minute break in the middle of the shift. I could either down a candy bar and a Coke from the vending machines in the breakroom or run to the Wilson Quick drugstore next door, which had a soda fountain and served hamburgers and cold drinks all the way up to closing time. The only problem was most of the time the counter was maintained by an ancient, shriveled specimen of a woman named Helen, who looked like an end-of-the-line version of Bette Davis. Old and crochety, she had only two speeds, slow and slower. If you made it to the drugstore in time and someone had an order in front of you or for some reason you got on Helen's bad side, you were doomed to leave hungry.

I drove to work that afternoon excited and proud that I'd be parking my new car on the hill where all my fellow workers could see it, where I could gaze up at it each time I came out of the store with an order to load in a car, knowing it would be waiting for me at shift's end. It was wonderful to have the feeling that on this night when I clocked out, I wouldn't need to ask someone to give me a ride home or worse, have to call my parents to come and pick me up. No, tonight I could punch the clock and stroll out the doors to my own vehicle. I could unlock the door under the moon and stars and the glow of the parking lot lights and slide in under the steering wheel of my very own 1962 Chevrolet Impala. Independence Day had arrived.

On my fourth trip outside to load some groceries into a customer's car, I cast my eyes toward my shiny car on the hill. I had to blink two or three times to make sure I was seeing what I was not seeing. Lo and behold, my 62 Chevy was gone. It was no longer where it had been just five minutes before. It was gone. I couldn't believe my eyes. Was someone playing a cruel joke on me?

No matter how desperately I tried to process what I was experiencing, the hard truth was my car was gone. No one was playing a trick on me. I was not imagining things. The car I had come to cherish in such a short time was not where it was supposed to be.

I ran back inside and told my boss that my car had been stolen. He called the police department and I called my father. Thirty minutes later, a police officer and my dad arrived at the store. The three of us walked up the hill to examine where my car had been parked. Nothing looked suspicious other than the fact that the car was gone. There was no broken glass or footprints or as my imagination ran wild, a left-behind ransom note for me to read.

> We have your car. Give us all the money
> from your upcoming paycheck and we will
> return it. If you delay, we will send it back
> to you one piece at a time.

The policeman filled out a report on a clipboard and I signed it. I was too sick to my stomach and depressed to go back to work, so my manager excused me, and I rode home with my dad. He was driving his service truck from Nashville Electric as I sat and looked out at the road before me. Everywhere I looked I thought for a brief moment I'd caught a glimpse of my car.

I stayed in my room that night feeling sorry for myself and wondering why God hated me so. Turning on my clock radio, I listened to some songs and did my best to keep from crying. "You're seventeen years old," I told myself. "You can't be crying over a car. You can't cry over anything anymore. Your dog can get hit by a truck or a pretty girl can say you're ugly and mean people can hotwire your car and steal it and sell it for parts and you still can't cry, because you're seventeen and you can't be a baby about such things. You have to grow up now. That's just the way it is."

I didn't sleep much that night and when I went to school the next morning, my heart wasn't in it. I couldn't stop thinking about some rotten thief driving my car somewhere around town.

It was one o'clock when a messenger from the school office came to my algebra class with a note from my dad. He was coming to the school to pick me up. My car had been found!

It wasn't the police who had located my car, but a man who worked at my store had managed to track it down. He'd just had a hunch, he told us, and when he looked behind a body shop, he found my beloved car sitting there by a dumpster. I didn't even know this fellow. He worked in the dairy department during the day while I was in school. But he'd heard all the commotion when he was leaving, and he had himself a hunch that he decided to follow up on.

To my surprise, there wasn't much wrong with my car. The thief had torn out the rubber seal around the window on the driver's side when he'd used a crowbar to get in. He took the same crowbar and knocked the ignition piece from the steering column so he could hotwire it. The chrome from the ignition lay in pieces on the floormat. Mr. Hinton thought maybe the cops get could dust for prints. That was his name. Mr. Hinton. Every day for the next two years, I went back to the dairy department and said hello to Mr. Hinton as I was coming and he was going. He would always ask, "How's that car doing?"

In fact, my car did fine for the rest of high school and my first two years of college. I took it to church camp three years in a row and fell in love with a college girl five years older than I. I also lived with its one eccentricity—when I went on any trip more fifty miles, the Impala became beset by vapor lock and shut off. As a result, I would have to sit on the side of the road for thirty minutes or so until it was ready to start back up again. It wasn't so bad once I got used to it. Sometimes I would be on a date when it would simply choose a place to shut down which would become our place to park. On a number of occasions, the choices my Chevy made were more original than mine.

On a summer night after my freshman year of college, I clocked out and drove down the street to buy burgers and fries for my friends who were still working. We would always eat in the parking lot after we all got off work and laugh and joke for an hour or so before heading home for the night. It was a little like having a Saturday night party. The grocery store's front walk was lined with new lawnmowers, bins of watermelons, barbeque grills, hanging plants, and other displays to entice the customers to get into a summer mode and spend all their money. I saw two guys rolling a lawnmower down the walkway, toward a waiting pickup truck. I knew they were in the process of stealing it, so I punched the accelerator and drove up on the sidewalk to cut them off, scraping the bottom of the Chevy with a sickening crunch. The men ran to their truck and roared away. The lawnmower was saved, but I shuddered to think what was wrong with my car.

The mechanic said it was my universal joint and replaced it. From then on, whenever I began to accelerate from a stop sign or green light, a knocking sound would come from beneath the floorboard—six or seven thuds, until the car's speed reached twenty miles an hour. Everyone heard it. It couldn't be ignored. I was also never able to find someone who could fix it. It would stop for a while and then come back with a renewed fury. I began to hear it, when it wasn't making the bumping sound at all, even in my sleep sometimes.

I finally put a "For Sale" sign on the windshield and parked it on the hill by the store. On the third day, a guy came in and wanted to know how much? He was a musician and played guitar in a combo. He thought maybe the Chevy could haul the band's trailer.

I sold the '62 Impala to him for three hundred dollars, half of what I paid for it. When the guitar player drove away, I didn't hear the knocking sound at all. Go figure. I thought about the three hundred I got for it compared to the six hundred I'd spent. It worked out to about a hundred dollars a year, a small price to pay for three exhilarating years of freedom.

2 Love at First Ride

Anthony Cavender

IN THE SUMMER OF 1958, when I was ten, I went on a ride in the foothills of the Sierra Nevada with my older brother, Doyle, in his Austin Healey 100–6. It was exhilarating. I had never ridden in a convertible. The experience opened an entirely new automotive world of wind, sky, immediacy, and freedom. Having ridden only in American barges, the Healey was dramatically different. I liked its smallness, snug seats, and dashboard display. It was nimble. It hugged the road and turned on a dime. The sleek styling was jaunty and elegant. I fell in love with the whole concept of the British roadster.

Fast forward to 1965. I'm driving my first car, a mint green, two-door, 1963 Chevrolet Impala, a 283 with "three on a tree." It was a good-looking car. I made some modifications to it: replaced the two-barrel carburetor with a four-barrel, installed a floor shifter, and put on a set of red-line tires. Over time, I noticed an incurable, cancerous rust forming on the back fenders and in the trunk. My father and I learned later, much to our chagrin, that the car originally came from New York state, a land of snow and salt.

One day on my commute to Belmont College, while waiting at a traffic light, I spotted a Triumph GT6 in British racing green in a car lot on West End. After studying it at a distance, I decided to pull into the lot for a closer look. Test-driving the GT6 brought back fond memories of riding in my brother's 100–6. On my third visit, the dealer knew I was hooked. He described the GT6 as a "poor man's Jaguar." He said that it would always be in style because it was designed by Giovanni Michelotti. Giovanni who? I knew nothing about him, but later learned that he was one the guys who designed some classic Ferraris and Maseratis. The lines and fastback style of the GT6 were looking better by the moment.

In the process of haggling, the salesman played the rust card hard, but we managed to arrive at a doable deal for someone who had meager savings, was going to college, and had a part-time job. Looking back, it wasn't a smart thing to do, but I'm often not completely rational when it comes to cars.

Not long after securing the GT6, I got a ticket, my first ticket, for reckless driving. I was cruising the local car-hop, Shoney's, and the adjacent shopping center, making radical turns and circles and cutting dangerously in front of cars. More to the point, I was showing off. Since paying the fine would severely deplete my limited resources, I decided to take my chances in traffic court. In court, the policeman calmly and accurately described my reckless driving behavior, pointing out that I was an accident waiting to happen. He was right about everything. I deserved the ticket. But I was a truculent boy-man who enjoyed arguing about anything with anyone at any time. So when it was my turn to speak, I politely asked the judge if I could use the court's chalkboard. I rolled the chalkboard over next to the judge so that he could clearly see my depiction of the traffic patterns around the car-hop and shopping center while I presented my argument, as absurd as it was. The judge seemed amused by my audacity and a bit put off by my lack of maturity and poor judgment. Mercifully, he ended up cutting the fine in half which, for me, was a major victory.

Like other owners of British sports cars, I was dependent on a good mechanic. "My" mechanic was a guy I nicknamed "Shit, Baby." He had a garage in the Five Points section of East Nashville. "Shit, Baby" was a short, scruffy man, around thirty years old. He had the face of a beaver. He was always covered in grease and oil. I called him "Shit, Baby" because of exchanges like these:

> Me: Have you figured out what's wrong?
> SB: You've got a carburetor problem.

Me: Can you fix it?
SB: Shit, baby, if you've got the money, I can fix it.
Me: Can you change out these wheels?
SB: Shit, baby, you don't want to do that!

I later regretted not respecting "Shit, Baby's" knowledge of British sports cars. Early in my ownership of the GT6, he advised me to be sure to give the knock-offs on the wire wheels "a good whack" once a week because, if I didn't, the wheel would gradually work itself off the axle. Unfortunately, I was a dumbass and had to learn the hard way. One afternoon, while entering the congested Courthouse Square from the Woodland Street bridge, I noticed a wobble in the left, front wheel and then heard a "clunk." The wheel was barely on and leaning inward. I had no choice but to jack up the car in the middle of the busy intersection and secure the wheel. Fortunately, a kind stranger helped by directing traffic. If you owned a British sports car in those days, you had to depend on the kindness of strangers.

There was another occasion when I was driving down I-40 to Knoxville and smoke began billowing out from under the dash. The needle on the temperature gauge was in the hot zone. A few seconds later the smoke was so thick that I couldn't see out of the windshield. I blindly negotiated the car to the side of the road and after the engine cooled down, I checked the radiator and found that it still had sufficient coolant. The oil level was also good. I was dumbfounded. I decided to walk to a nearby service station just off the Gordonsville exit.

When I walked into the garage all the country boy mechanics stared at me for the oddity I was: a crazy hippie. I had a moustache with long, red hair down to my shoulders, a sweated leather hat was perched on my head, and I wore a loud, floral shirt with billowed sleeves and bell-bottom pants. The owner of the garage, a burly man of few words named Nick, drove me back to the car in his wrecker. He quickly surmised that I had a stuck thermostat. He detached the hose leading from the radiator into the engine and pulled out the thermostat with a screwdriver. After inspecting it, he flung it into the brush. "You'll be alright to get to Knoxville, but get you a new thermostat soon." I thanked him and asked how much I owed him for his work. "Five dollars," he said. He deserved more. That's the best five dollars I ever spent in my life. Like I said, the kindness of strangers. Thereafter, whenever I drove to Knoxville, I always stopped at that service station to fill up and say hello to Nick. He and I became friends...sort of.

I was tiring of "Shit, Baby's" smartass manner when I was told about another garage near Vanderbilt, Elrod's, that specialized in foreign cars. Elrod did several jobs for me. I remember his replacing a universal joint and tachometer cable and repairing the wiper motor. He resolved other niggling issues that plagued most British sports cars of that era, including mine.

Elrod was in his late sixties, tall, skinny, and, unlike "Shit, Baby," congenial. There was a sign on the wall outside his garage that read "If You Can't Stop, Smile as You Drive By." His overalls and pen-striped shirts were always clean. On a wall in his office hung a black and white photograph, yellowed with age, taken of him right after he was born. It was the tiniest baby I'd ever seen. He weighed only 14 ounces at birth. "The doctors all said I wouldn't survive, but here I am," he'd say with a smile to everyone who asked about the picture. He told me he displayed the picture because he was living proof that miracles really do happen.

Elrod was also a first-rate mechanic even though I remember him as something of a human sloth. He spoke slowly, walked slowly, ate slowly, and worked on cars slowly. His slow work at times put me in the vexing situation of locating rides to school and work. I knew I needed something more reliable. Still, I kept the GT6 for three years and finally sold it to my nephew after which I purchased another American barge, a Plymouth Satellite, from my father.

Years later, I came full circle. I bought a 1967 Austin Healey 3000 BJ8. When I got behind its wheel, the glorious memory of riding in my brother's 100–6 washed over me. As far as I am concerned, the 3000 is and forever will be the ultimate driving machine. I had few problems maintaining it. It's the only car I've owned that I didn't lose money on. Unfortunately, I had to sell it to remain in graduate school. I could not quite make it on the paltry stipend of a teaching assistantship, a minuscule scholarship, and painting houses on the side.

Now, many miles down the road, I drive a car ironically described as "a poor man's 911": a Porsche Boxster. Auto enthusiasts say that it handles as well if not better than a 911. It's the best engineered car I've driven by far. It's very Teutonic: durable, reliable, efficient, and functional. It's extraordinarily nimble, so much so that you find yourself comfortably driving over a 100 and not worrying about a thing except for the idiots in the other cars around you and, of course, the state troopers. You're encourage to take risks that you normally wouldn't take. It's happy on the Autobahn and touring the mountains of East Tennessee. The Boxster saved the Porsche company financially, and it saved me from a life of boring driving. The Boxster is in many ways, the latest and greatest, but whether ten years old or retired as I now am, I would still choose the 3000 Austin Healy in a heartbeat.

3 My Horseless Carriage

Tom Burton

I'M APPROACHING NINETY YEARS of age, and I've only bought one car new—my 1966 convertible MG Midget. It was a tribute to myself for a race won, like a collar of roses for the wins of Man of War or Seabiscuit. My victory was a terminal degree run against a premier Southern University with overwhelming odds. The day before I purchased the car, I had talked to the owner of the dealership, and he said he could not take less than $2200. When I returned the following day, the salesman (whom I later learned was the owner's son) said I could have it for $2100. I told him what the owner had said, and he agreed go back inside and try to get a lower price. When he came outside, he said he had indeed persuaded the owner to take only $2150. I was pleased to get the special deal and bought the car. I'm not sure if that were a prophetic "sign" of the sagacity or the lack thereof. My MG was not the car that a colleague of mine received when I was teaching in a small high school before pursing the terminal degree—his car was the gift of his brother, singer Pat Boone, who drove up in the parking lot to present him the keys to a new Jaguar. Regardless, my car was after all British too, and I knew I would be really cool going every day to my personal university reserved parking space, which then had my last name painted on the curb (unlike now with parking permits at a premium charge).

Cars need a name, like their forebearers, horses: the mythical winged Pegasus, Southern icons Traveller and Little Sorrel, movie stars Champion and Trigger, and my very own horse when I was six years old, a white mare that I inspiringly named Silver. But I didn't get to name my horseless carriage, it was named for me by a friend—the Sopwith Camel—not from the pages of heroic WWI aerial history, but from the *Peanuts* dogfights of Snoopy and the Red Baron. I'm not sure whether the name was to depict the car or the driver. Nevertheless, my trusty MG and I flew well together. It was new and needed little maintenance, which I could do myself: change plugs, points, and condensers, even adjust valves. I would eventually ride long distances in it, such as to Texas and south Florida. On one trip to Texas, at night in the rain being passed by eighteen wheelers, I kept imagining skidding like Steve McQueen completely through the space between the front and rear tires of the trailers. Even if I had, I wouldn't have been able to observe it because the windshield wipers were more metronomes than wipers.

But I came nigh to losing the Sopwith Camel on the occasion of a divorce. Fortunately, the settlement for me was two items: my MG and a bedroll. A friend of mine and I drove the Sopwith Camel to his lifelong friend's residence, a one-bedroom and kitchenette apartment. My friend's friend came to the door and replied to my request for housing, "*Mi casa es tu casa.*" It was a symbiotic relationship. I didn't have a roof over my head except a canvas one, and he didn't have a car, but he did have an army cot that my bedroll fit perfectly. At that point the MG became more than a sportive ride; it took on the character of a pack-horse, weekly trips from our apartment to the grocery, laundromat, etc. One incident during that period was the MG's finest hour. It was winter during a big snow storm, my friend's divorced wife and four kids (ages eleven to fifteen) were marooned in a trailer outside town with no heat, food, or transportation. Of course, the MG, friend, and I went to the rescue. We made it there with little trouble, but the snow kept getting deeper. When we arrived at the trailer, we packed everything into the MG: the three larger children on the shelf behind the bucket seats, one child on the gear hump between the seats, my friend in the rider's bucket seat with divorced wife on his lap holding a cat and a gallon of milk. The MG had the traction of a tank.

Much later on, I had another car and was not quite as naïve as when I purchased the MG; therefore, I thought it would be a bonding act to give the MG to one of my sons. He enjoyed doing power turns and other skillful NASCAR maneuvers, but he didn't understand that an owner of a MG Midget has to have an empathetic oneness with the idiosyncrasies of the machine, much as with a horse that can be ridden hard, not winded, not put up wet, etc. Unfortunately, my son didn't have that Buddhist perspective. He probably hadn't even read the *Black Stallion*. When the car refused to perform, he released it in an adjoining weeded field under a rotten tarp to rust and rust and rust.

Nevertheless, I retrieved the car and began the process of healing, binding, and recovery—unfortunately, without the benefit of Medicare. So now, carefully groomed in its stall, though no longer racing or even holding well all its fluids and needing implants of several internal parts, my MG Midget furnishes me significant memories of important periods of my life and still gives me pleasure during our Sunday afternoon rides together.

4 Mabel's Driving Rules

Roberta T. Herrin

IN 1945, AT THE end of World War II, my father Lee was sent to the Philippines with the US Army. He left behind his father, my mother, and four children on their east Tennessee farm, high in the mountains, isolated at the head of a holler on a dirt road. Their self-sufficiency was legendary. They bought very little except for a few staples, such as flour, sugar, coffee, and salt. They had always managed without any sort of vehicle, but in my father's absence, my mother Mabel was responsible not only for her children but also her 78-year-old father-in-law. She needed transportation, so she asked her stepfather to find a good, affordable car. He obliged and found a 78-horsepower, flathead V-8 1935 Ford coupe with a rumble seat. Though it was ten years old, he assured her that it was well maintained and stout. It could "take" the mountain's steep dirt roads, potholes, and mud, especially when the spring thaw and rains turned the roads into thick, brown muck.

She bought the car sight unseen. Her two younger brothers, Hoover and Earl, drove it up the mountain from Elizabethton and left her to master it. My mother was 34 years old and ignorant about cars. My brother Zane was 12. With him in the passenger seat, she drove around and through the hilly pasture, learning to shift gears and steer. To further hone her skills, she drove through the apple orchard, yard, and around the weatherboard house. Here, the Ford got the better of her, and she crashed into the side of the house. The "stout" car was undamaged; the house did not fare so well.

In 1945 few people on the mountain owned a car, and there were NO women drivers. Mabel became both famous and infamous: What business did a woman have driving a car? (Never mind their roles in WWII.) My father was a quiet man, so I have no idea what he thought of his independent wife. What was it like for him to come home from the War to a woman who had bought a car, learned to drive, and had become the de facto taxi for the neighbors, taking them to the doctor, to buy groceries, to cash welfare checks, and picking up hitchhikers, who were plentiful in those days?

What I do know is that my father had a deep appreciation for cars—their design, their engines, their power, and their beauty— but he was strictly a Ford man. After Mabel's first 1935 Ford, all our cars were HIS cars, and HE kept them spotless—immaculate. No eating, no drinking, no stringing out our chewing gum in the car. No litter. He washed and polished the car weekly. Annually, the county paved sections of road with a gooey black tar that stuck to everything—it was nothing like today's asphalt—and my father spent hours using kerosene to clean it off the sides, the underneath, and the wheels. Mabel, on the other hand, never washed the car or waxed it or cleaned the interior. For her, the car was strictly utilitarian.

The first car I remember was a 1949 Ford coupe. I was born in 1949, so my memory of it is dim. I remember more clearly the 1954 Ford sedan that replaced it and my mother's ire when Daddy "traded cars." She was practical. Why did we need a new car? It proved itself, however, to be another good, stout car. In the winter, there were no snow plows, but it conquered the ice and subdued deep drifts. Mabel often put us in the back seat to improve traction. If that didn't work, she put chains on the tires.

Whatever she thought of the 1954 Ford, she drove it expertly on the winding mountain roads. In those days, even the main roads, such as highway 19E between Roan Mountain and Elizabethton, were narrow, crooked things with one-lane bridges that had their own rules and etiquette. I remember sliding lower and lower in the back seat of the Ford while Mabel faced off a tractor and trailer on the one-lane bridge near my uncle Coon Miller's store. She got to the bridge first and had every right to enter it when a huge semi came barreling through. They met half-way, nose to nose, and she refused to back up. The truck driver rolled down his window and shouted obscenities and waved her backwards. She wouldn't budge. As he slowly retreated (not an easy feat because the road paralleled both sides of the river and the bridge crossed at right angles), Mabel eased the car forward, and when we passed by his window, she never looked at him, did not shout obscenities in his direction, but drove serenely forward. To this day, I can see the driver's red face hanging out the window and hear him shout, "Lady, I'm gonna paint this thang red so next time you can SEE it." Scrunched low on the floor behind the front seat, I thought, *Buster, you are a self-deluded man if you think that would help this situation.* She had principles.

Then Daddy bought a 1958 Ford Fairlane coupe with a V-8 engine, a four-barrel carburetor that generated 335 horsepower, dual exhausts, and power steering. It was red and white—and LONG—with sleek lines and a red and white interior. It was magnificent. It could fly. I thought it had wings. Daddy kept the Fairlane longer than usual, so long that Mama—not Daddy—taught me to drive it when I was 18. She never once mentioned its perfection and power; I never mentioned its artistry and style. As she taught me to navigate the twisting mountain roads, I realized that her appreciation for a car was different from Daddy's—sophisticated and complex. I have three older sisters, none of whom learned to drive until they were married and were taught by their husbands. I was fortunate to be taught by a woman who not only mastered the skill, but fathomed the special relationship among driver, car, and road, so much so that she articulated her own set of rules for the mastery. Her driving rules have stayed with me, eventually becoming a metaphor for living:

(1) Never look at what's coming toward you. As long as it stays on its side of the road, pay it no mind. She said, "We naturally

steer toward what we focus on, and if you look at an oncoming vehicle, you'll hit it." (2) Always look ahead to where you are going—to where you want to be; never focus on where you are. Do not focus on the road directly in front of the car you are driving. If you do, you'll be surprised by the curve up ahead. (3) Always speed up in the apex of the curve. It takes momentum and force to carry you through the arc. If you feel the need to slow down, apply the brakes before you enter the curve, never in the middle of it. (4) Don't work so hard. When the steering wheel feels heavy and easy in your hands, you will be in control. Feel what the road and the wheels tell you through the steering wheel and manage it with grace. I remember the exact spot where I felt for the first time that the steering wheel and the car and the road and I were in sync. It was lovely.

When I left for college in 1967, my parents gave me a car. I was just grateful to have any car and didn't expect a Mustang or a Thunderbird, but I did think it would be a Ford. I was wrong. My first car was a powder blue 1963 Plymouth Valiant with a push-button gear shift on the dashboard to the left of the steering wheel. Its slant-6 engine and 101 horsepower were the antithesis of a 1958 Ford V-8 with a four-barrel carburetor. But I drove that car for nine years, always using Mabel's driving rules, never wishing for a Mustang. Like my mother, I was practical and utilitarian. The Valiant became the de facto taxi for roommates and boyfriends. It took me home many weekends through snow and mud, and, like Mabel, I learned to put chains on the tires. The Valiant had its own charm and served me well, but the poor little thing could never match the 1958 Ford Fairlane. No car ever will. It captured my heart and inspired a love of engines, but mostly it taught me that a man and a woman can have different but oddly compatible notions about a car: one mechanical but aesthetic; the other utilitarian but philosophical. I came to understand that a car transcends its components when it is valued—cherished—for itself and for its unique contribution to a marriage, a family, a life.

5 A View from the Tailgate of an El Camino

Scott Braswell

For most folks old enough to remember, the Chevrolet El Camino probably represents a best-forgotten era of automotive experimentation. Not quite a car, not quite a truck--and not enough of either to earn the adoration of the auto-purchasing public--it eventually faded into obscurity, relegated to the ranks of car show curiosities and junkyards' rusted ruins.

But for my grandfather, the El Camino represented a kind of chocolate-meets-peanut butter miracle of automotive ingenuity. Up front: inconspicuous and respectable enough to occupy a curbside parking spot at Sunday service. In the back: a blue-collar build tailored for hauling all manner of transport: random heaps of trinkets culled from roadside rummages, or the kind of small-town auction houses where you could bid on a set of used riding lawnmower tires with one hand, and dig into a hot plate of fried pork rinds with the other – or a ramshackle go-kart, salvaged from a graveyard of abandoned lawnmower parts and reconfigured for the tireless delight of his oldest grandchild.

The English translation of El Camino is "The Way." I only learned this recently, but thinking back, the meaning fits. For a few sparkling summers that car was the way my grandfather and I connected, particularly when it came to fishing excursions. These endeavors always began with selecting a few simple and reliable tools of the trade: an old tacklebox filled with a splashy cast of lures--used and unused, some slim and salmon shaped, others boasting colorful frills and almost psychedelic paint jobs – a few well-worn rod-n-reel combos (Grandaddy was a Zebco man), a couple of cane poles (my personal preference), and a chain-link collapsible catfish net, decorated with the rust and algae of previous excursions.

Of course, bait was also essential, and there were typically two options. One, Catawba worms, which are kind of like the muscle car of caterpillars – sleek and black, with yellow pinstripes running down the sides, and also happen to be a favorite cuisine for catfish. Whenever possible we would use the before-mentioned cane poles to knock the bait-to-be down from the long backyard limbs of catalpa trees sprouting behind Grandaddy's garden. I can only imagine what inquisitive neighbors thought while watching these shenanigans, but we would continue to slap the tree limbs with vigor until we had enough worms to justify a fishing trip.

On less successful days, when the Catawba's seemed savvy to our scheme, we would turn to the second, backup bait option, which required pulling into a ramshackle gas station on the outskirts of town to pick up a prepared-by-hand collection of garden variety earthworms, usually packaged in repurposed cream cheese containers. During these roadside stops, we'd find a gaggle of belt-buckled and booted farmers milling around outside the storefront, debating – between cigarette tokes – the lifespan of an old Snapper lawnmower that was seeking refuge at an adjoining small engine repair shop.

We would walk beneath a weathered sign decorating the entrance that read "Ice Cold Brrrrr!" in pale blue letters. And inside, Grandaddy would select a container of bait from the store's humming fridge, its tired motor straining to keep the summer heat at bay. He would then exchange pleasantries with a suspendered clerk, who dangled a cigarette between his fingers while he talked, his words half-obscured by the crackle of the old pocket radio perched on top of his cash register. It was my job to retrieve a couple of cold bottles of Coca-Cola (Fanta Grape for me, if it was in stock), from the machine in the back of the store. The dispenser in question was duotone (red and white), with a slim glass front door showcasing the caps of the available selections. I would retrieve two bottles and slide them on to the countertop next to the bait. Grandaddy would drop a few wrinkled bills on the counter and exchange farewells with the clerk. Ring of the register, jingle of the doorbell, and we'd be off. The El Camino would kick up a cloud of red clay dust as I watched the old farmers, still engaged in heated debate, disappear in the rearview.

Enroute to our destination, we'd rip along sunbaked rural backroads, a rush of pines whipping by, the thick summer air pushing through open windows. Grandaddy would occasionally croon along to the AM crackle of local country radio, his voice drifting endearingly in and out of key.

I rarely knew where we were going during those outings, but I do remember that, aside from the two-lane byways of Butts County, few actual roads were involved in accessing our destination. With his left elbow resting on the open window, and right hand palming the steering wheel, Grandaddy would suddenly recognize a landmark, a property line, or some mysterious indicator known only to him, and do his patented one-hand turn – spinning the steering wheel with his palm down and fingers up – and tear away from the main two-lane onto either an open field with no clear path or into a thickly wooded area with only a slim semblance of a throughway. After enduring the scratch and scrape sounds of thickets and pine branches beating the sides of the El Camino, and feeling some concern for our location and our safety, my anxiety would quickly subside as – inevitably – a shimmering pond would materialize, seemingly out of the ether. Approaching the water, Grandaddy had an odd habit of cutting the engine before coming to a complete stop. He would speed up a bit, turn the engine off, and wait a few beats before throwing the gearshift into park. The rumble of the El Camino's engine would fall silent, trading places with a swelling chorus of cicadas – a certified staple of a southern summer.

I remember vividly sitting on that car's tailgate, my small legs dangling off the edge, and watching shadows of clouds roll across a sea of tall field grass while my grandfather prepared the rod and reels and did his best to ensure that the coming evening's fish fry wouldn't leave dinner plates empty.

I don't remember many words being exchanged during these episodes, but few were necessary. Whether it was fishing, or "taking a spin" to the post office ("the P.O."), or to the church parking lot with the go-kart loaded in the back of the El Camino, and Grandaddy being kind enough to provide fuel for a half-hour's worth of figure 8's on the hot asphalt until the little Briggs & Stratton gas tank went from full to fumes. Whatever it was, wherever the destination, I was just happy to be along for the ride.

But time moved on.

The years waved goodbye to one another, and the El Camino watched its workload diminish. A well-earned rest after so many years of dutiful service.

One summer when I was much older, during a visit to Jackson, I noticed that my grandfather's faithful companion had taken on the ravages of time. The lines in its face were deeper, and its body wore the scars of a long and useful life – a cracked headlight, a dented fender, a tailgate pock-marked by rust, a severely wounded sideview mirror hanging on for dear life, and enough mysterious cracks, scuffs, and divots to spark a hundred theories as to their origins.

At one point, I noticed that the "El Camino" logo had fallen off the vehicle's front quarter panel. For whatever reason, the thought came to me, "The old car finally let it go." It had laid down its mantle, turned in its badge, and turned off its "Open for Service" lights. As we all must do, at some point. I picked up the ornament and washed it off in an old basin my grandfather used to use to dress his fish. Satisfied with a semblance of its old chrome sheen, I hoisted it up high and propped it against a cracked pane of glass inside my grandfather's woodshop, hoping that the setting sun, which had begun its slow slide down the Georgia skyline, would now see it clearly and restore some of its shimmer, if only for a few moments more.

6 Viva the Vega and Other Cars I Loved

Don Harris

I HAVE FOND MEMORIES of growing up in Upper East Tennessee during the 1970's and 80's. Several of the memories that make me smile to this day involved cars. I was lucky because my dad was what was known in those days as a "car man." He worked for several major American and foreign car dealers and eventually owned his own dealership. As long as I can remember, I have always harbored a fascination with anything on wheels that could be peddled, throttled, or even released by hand to propel one down a long hill until the rider had to jump off or suffer another skinned knee or elbow. From banana bikes to skateboards, I loved them all.

I can remember how my dad was always bringing home the latest "demo" from his lot which was always a model that had some power and stylish looks. By the time I was in my early teens, I had somewhat of an in-depth knowledge of both the product line for whatever manufacturer or dealership he was representing at the time, as well as how the automobile sales business operated. I started working the normal neighborhood jobs when I turned fourteen, including mowing lawns, bailing hay and yes – even babysitting. These various jobs helped me save a little coin in my own personal Folgers can that I kept on the top shelf of my closet. When I turned fifteen, I felt like I hit the mother-load of all jobs when my Dad asked me if I wanted the car washing job at the dealership where he was the General Manager. It was a Chrysler / Dodge dealership and looking back, I realize how radically times have changed in comparison to how dealers keep their cars clean in the 21st century. Back then, on any given summer day or weekend, all you had to do was follow the rubber water hose into any one of the rows where new or used cars were parked, and look for the puddle of water. I would be somewhere on one of the two sides of the car with a long-handled brush and a five-gallon bucket of car wash soap. My Dad even ordered me the MOPAR dealer shirt that I proudly wore, the one like the mechanics in back all wore with my name printed on the left chest. Today, go to almost any dealership and you will see that they have automated wash systems where cars are run through and washed within seconds. I still like to think in my selective memory, that despite being slower, the cars I washed were much cleaner!

Back to my Folgers can and the fact that the more I worked, the larger the lettuce pile inside that can became. In case you might be thinking that my parents didn't teach me about savings accounts and interest earnings, I did have to deposit a portion of each check into a savings account every two weeks. As I approached my 16th birthday, I kept pestering my dad that I wanted a car to go back and forth to school, basketball practice and to work in. He would always respond that he would start looking for the right car for me and that I would have to pay half of the cost of whatever he found from my savings. Of course, my imagination ran wild, and the anticipation of what my own set of wheels would actually look like was killing me. I was already getting valuable driving experience moving the new and used cars around the sales lot on a regular basis and driving the family car up and down the dead-end street that we lived on. I can still recall that blustery December day in 1977 as if it was yesterday. I remember him coming home for dinner and telling me that he had found the perfect used car for me. He said it was a Chevy and left it at that. Now let me tell you, we lived somewhat close to the Bristol Motor Speedway and I attended the NASCAR Winston Cup Series race every spring, and knew something about every racer on the circuit and the cars they drove.

When I heard my dad say Chevy, I was thinking Monte Carlo or maybe a Nova or even an Impala. The next day was a Saturday when my Dad pulled into the driveway that afternoon driving a 1974 gold Chevrolet Vega Hatchback. As I came out the garage door from the basement, I saw it sitting there and thought it must belong to one of my mom's or sister's friends. Walking down to the driveway, I still can hear Dad say, "So how do you like it, son"? I must admit that it was a lot smaller and had less horsepower than I wanted, but it was a car and it looked brand new. He said, "Gimme $750 and you can call it yours."

I jumped in the all-black interior with bucket seats and headed down our street. I was sold hook, line and sinker and felt like my dad had just handed me the keys to freedom. My best friend had also just gotten a Ford Pinto hatchback and we would debate which car was better. In reality, it was like arguing which food is more gourmet – a grilled cheese sandwich or a cheeseburger? In other words, we were totally oblivious regarding the fact that we were both driving the bottom feeders of the American auto industry. Life seemed more innocent in those days.

I took my first "road trip" with my two best friends in the Vega. We drove down to Hotlanta to watch a Braves game and after the game, there was a nightclub in downtown Atlanta that was calling our name. We wanted to see what the disco life was like. As we pulled in to the club parking lot, I realized there was valet parking. I remember pulling in and tossing my keys to the valet as we started towards the entrance. I didn't know why the guy was laughing at the time, but today can imagine how three hay-seed, wet behind the ears teenagers must have looked pulling into that urban nightclub in a Gold Vega wearing jeans, t-shirts and suede chukka - boots.

In any event, I took care of that Vega like it was a Lincoln Continental. My Dad took notice and one day after about a year of driving the Vega, he asked me if I would like to drive something else. In hindsight, I realize he probably had a customer who he thought he could sell my car to and make a profit. But when he told me it was a 240 Z, I became totally pumped. It was a white hatchback with raised white letter Goodyear tires and an auto-matic transmission. It had been wrecked on the front end, but was allegedly repaired. I forget how much I paid for the difference with the trade-in, but during that spring of my 17th year, I felt like Paul Newman driving around Johnson City and adjoining locales. I must admit that I had quite a lead foot which led to me being gifted my first speeding ticket. I believe the ticket was in the $50 dollar range – pretty hefty for those days. There was one unforeseen problem with the car which I began to notice in late spring, when I had to roll the windows up to turn on the AC. Evidently, the former accident resulted in the car being a little off-frame. As a result, the rear hatch lid didn't completely seal when shut, allowing the exhaust from the tailpipe to seep into the rear of the car. We tried to adjust it several times, but it never would fully seal.

The last time it was supposedly fixed, I had a date with a new girl at our high school to go see a concert in Knoxville. I still remember picking her up in my little sports car. Pulling out of the driveway and heading to a concert in a distant town with a good-looking coed, I felt like I was James Bond driving in Monte Carlo. We had a great night of fun, but like the saying goes – all good things must come to an end. On our way home, as she was sitting next to me looking through my clunky 8 track tapes, she started to complain that she had a headache and felt like she was going to throw up. When we finally arrived at her home, she opened the door and ran into the house—no goodnight kiss or anything. Disappointed, I headed home and felt a little light-headed myself. Bright and early the next morning, her mom called to tell my mother that her daughter had experienced carbon monoxide poisoning and had to be taken to the hospital. Her mother said she was going to be all right, but asked what could have happened. I knew that at that point, the car was never going to be fixed, so I asked my dad to help me sell it.

Within a couple of weeks, he told me to come out to the lot and find something. I remember pulling up and spotting a used 1974 Dodge Charger. It looked just like the one Richard Petty drove, with a stripe streaming down each side of a long hood and elevated tail. I told my dad that was the one I wanted and to this day, I know he took a loss on that car so that I could afford it. Much appreciated, Pop.

That car was the "Bomb" for me and I can remember how clean I kept it. Remember, this was my third car in less than 18 months, but it still felt like my first car. I am a Dodge person and to this day still try to own at least one Dodge or Chrysler product in our family's small stable of vehicles. I do believe that I went a little overboard with my love and upkeep of the Charger. Even as I enter my later years, I still cannot stand a dirty car, either on the outside or interior.

This behavior became manifest early as a result of an embarrassing incident on one of my dates in high school. I was taking out one of my sister's friends whose father was a physician in town. It was raining that night as we headed to the movies. I remember when walking her to my car, she took a shortcut through her yard that had just been sodded to avoid the rain. I stayed on the front entrance path to the driveway and caught up with her at the passenger door. Opening the passenger door, I looked down and noticed that her shoes were muddy and wet. She got in and as I walked around the back, I was thinking that she needs to keep her feet on the floor mats. When I opened my door, I noticed that her left foot was on the carpet between the two mats. That sent shivers down my "Mr. Clean" spine and I must have blurted out that from that point forward, she needed to keep her feet on the floor mat in order to avoid mud stains. She laughed and said that everything washes out. I just shook my head and off we went. The next day, she told my sister that she felt like she was on a date with an elementary school teacher who watched her every move. That led to my mom eventually reading me the riot act for not being a total gentleman and valuing my old car over another person's feelings. I did eventually call her to apologize and learned an important lesson that night. The first love you experience with your car can make you act irrational on occasion. Almost everyone looks back at their first car with fond memories and may even tell you down to the smallest detail, what the car looked like, crazy road trips taken, and the day that you got rid of it. Here's to all of those wonderful memories with the hope that future American teens will be able to experience something similar.

7 Mustang Sally

Michael Braswell

MY FIRST CAR WAS a 1959 Chevy Bel Air, six-cylinder, straight drive two-door coupe. While the two-door coupe sounds pretty good, the gull wings, two-tone paint and six-cylinder engine landed me at the rear of the Saturday night Dairy Queen parade. Jimmy T's GTO and Nate's Daddy's T-Bird were the stuff of dreams, tickling the fantasies of high school girls who batted their eyelashes and waved excitedly as the drivers passed by. They were mesmerized by the manly beauty of the cars, imagining Cary Grant, James Dean, or some other Hollywood icon behind the wheel rather that the pimple-faced drivers grinning back at them. Still, the Chevy was a big step up from the three-speed Schwinn. While there were no small-town beauties eager to climb in, there was room enough for me, Bert, C.M. and Bobby to cruise around sucking on milkshakes and talking trash about what we saw that was still out of our reach. While our dreams and fantasies were really no different from Nate's and Jimmy D's, they had the hypnotic rides that were catnip to teenage girls and we didn't. If only . . .

If my father had owned a car and truck dealership rather than a jewelry store, there is no doubt in my mind that I would have never seen the inside of a classroom. As grateful as I am to have enjoyed (for the most part) a long teaching vocation, I would have been a car and truck man. Hustling sales, appraising vehicles, and cruising around in the latest and greatest rides would have most likely been my lot in life. What kind of car man would I have been? Would I have been like the overweight sales manager with a peroxide blonde curly perm, dressed in a lime green leisure suit sporting a fake gold nugget ring on each hand at a Chevy dealership, trying to sell me a used Astro van? I hope not. Intellectual introspection and ethical maturity are not priorities in the car and truck business. Service awards on gilded plaques hanging on office walls claim that service to customers is the dealer's number one priority, but truth be told, it is instead about how often car dealers can get them to bring their cars and trucks in for service and how much money can be made off those services.

"No payments until next year," "free Christmas cash," "tires for life," and "200,000 mile transmission warranties," are the bait they cast out to nervous and excited customers, tempting them to come closer, but not too close to read the fine print. On occasion, they will even throw out a marketing trawler net offering free three-night cruises to the Bahamas or weekend getaways to Dollywood - anything to lure them into the den of the finance and insurance manager for a game of add-on and upgrades roulette. I hope I would have been one of the good guys, helping folks to buy what they could afford and making a decent living for the effort, but as the Good Book says, "The Spirit is willing, but the flesh is weak." Fortunately, that was not to be my vocational destiny and I am glad of it. Still, like my father before me, I have held a keen interest in cars and trucks, starting with my old '59 two-door Chevy.

I put my two-tone beauty through its paces until I went off to college in 1965. As a university freshman, I rode the city buses like other first-year students until I inherited my mother's four-cylinder Pontiac Tempest station wagon. The Tempest was at best, a half-step above my old Chevy. At every stop, it had a rough idle, requiring a turn of the ignition key more often than not. It was better than the city bus, but not by much. Then in September of 1966, if memory serves me right, a miracle happened.

Standing with my father in the used car lot of Moultrie's Ford dealership, the clouds departed and a heavenly light beamed down upon us as we stood before a 289 four-barrel V-8, steel blue 1965 Ford Mustang with blue vinyl bucket seats and an automatic floor shifter. From then on, my car time was measured in BM (before Mustang) and AM (after Mustang). No man could give a greater gift to his son than my father gave to me on that day. For $1995 plus tax, he and I drove home with my very own Mustang and I drove into a future of unlimited possibilities both good and bad.

That Christmas I completed my dream machine by spending $50 for four Mag wheel-covers and twenty dollars for Mr. Holland, a family friend who owned an upholstery business, to make a blue vinyl matching cushion that fit on the hump between the two front bucket seats. I can still remember driving back to college, listening to Otis Redding, Sam and Dave, and one of my favorites, Wilson Pickett belting out "Mustang Sally." Let the games begin.

Unfortunately, there was an inverse relationship between my burgeoning social life and my declining academic performance. Road trips, being elected social chairman of my fraternity, and romance, all contributed in various ways to a pitiful grade point average that placed me a whisper away from academic probation or worse, suspension which earned me the ire of my parents replete with lamentations regarding the poor example I was setting for my three younger brothers.

No doubt I knew better, but the siren's voice was strong and like Willie Nelson crooned years later, it always felt good for me and my buddies to be on the road again. Like the time, Jeff and I traveled from Macon to New Orleans two weekends in a row to experience its forbidden lure. I rounded up all my available cash and Jeff sold his coin collection to fund our sojourn. We set out on our adventure with two other friends in our chariot, Jeff's Volkswagen Beetle. Exceeding the speed limit along the Mississippi coast in Biloxi, we were stopped by the local gendarmes and taken to the home of the Justice of the Peace where we were fined seventy dollars. Eyeing his garage stacked high with cases of beer and knowing the age limit in Mississippi was 18, we inquired about the possibility of purchasing a case of Pabst Blue Ribbon which he readily agreed to. His parting words to us as we loaded the beer into the car was, "You boys drive safe, now."

After settling into a local budget hotel, we got lucky and procured dates for Saturday night from a nearby girls' college. Eight people in a VW Beetle cruising down Bourbon Street was quite a sight to see. The girls invited us to return the following week for the start of Mardi Gras which made perfect sense to us. Missing most of two weeks of class—what could go wrong?

Weekend soirees and parties, midweek gatherings to finish off what was left from the weekend, intramural sports, and part-time jobs to finance said activities, left little time for class attendance and study. And creative bullshit no matter how imaginative, only went so far in writing essays on subjects in history, philosophy and psychology one knew little about. Academically speaking, dark clouds continued to gather on what I hoped, was the distant horizon.

Games among buddies and frat brothers constituted the upside of college life. Big talk, card games, road trips, sports, and all manner of other normal and on occasion, abnormal, activities comprised the bone and muscle of young men interacting with other guys were one thing. Games of the heart were another matter. As in high school, only more intensely, hurts were given and received. Folks fell in and out of love, sometimes falling too deep to climb out of the place where relationships end. Regrets - what one said or should have said to a friend long passed or how one treated a stranger, are remembered in old age. Romantic break-ups can be hard whether gradual or sudden. Emotions run strong and maturity and sensitivity are often lacking. I could have said, should have said, would have said . . . Whatever the games, realities, or outcomes during college years, one tends to soldier on, thinking more about what's around the next bend than what is left behind.

After my academic suspension near miss, I hit the road with Mustang Sally a bit less and studied a bit more. Trouble was, I had cut all the easy classes and electives with the dismal grades to show for it. All I had left were the hard courses like statistics taught by the infamous math department, the "Darth Vader" of my college curriculum.

Leaving class with my buddy, Larry, he uttered the fateful words, "That's the girl I was telling you about." I looked at the girl walking down the sidewalk twenty yards away and realized I had her confused with someone else. It turned out she was in summer school so she could graduate early, while I was there for the second summer in a row to make up my ill-fated D's and F's. She had been on campus the entire time I had been there and during the last part of the last semester, I by chance, happened to see her walking from class.

When you meet someone who is pleasing to your eye and touch, and for one reason or another, you trust, the odds are that something good may be in the offing. Perhaps, in time, two may become one and even the possibility of lifelong intimacy and partnership, and who knows what else?

I knew I was on the precipice, looking at a future I had seen in too many Holliday Inn bars, middle-aged sales reps drinking too much and bemoaning this or that thing about their lives. Could I pull a rabbit out of a hat, and somehow get myself into graduate school, maybe even become a teacher like I always hoped to be. Still, with a 1.9 grade point average after two years of college, it would be a long-shot. But maybe . . .

8 Hello, Goodbye

Ralph Bland

IN THE SPRING OF 1972, I should have been making plans to graduate from college, but since I had to work and pay my own way through school, I didn't quite have enough hours to graduate. With the Viet Nam War coming to an end, and since I had nothing but the rest of my life to look forward to anyway, the decision was fairly simple. I would stay another year and graduate in 1973. In the meantime, I planned to party down my senior year and start worrying about the future after that. Starting that fall, I would devote myself to taking only classes I liked and continue working in order to stay afloat financially, thus freeing myself up to chase after the girls on campus with whom I figured I might get lucky. I would finish the year, take the summer off, and come back in the fall rip-roaring to go.

The first order of business was finding a new car. I'd owned a 1962 Chevy Impala my first three years of college and while it was a fine first automobile, it was beginning to go south on me mechanically. That fact coupled with my male ego wanting something more dashing and sexy, I put it on the block and sold it. I drove my dad's stripped-down Pontiac Tempest for a month or so while I looked for a car. He wanted me to buy a car from my uncle's son—a Karman Ghia—but my cousin wanted too much for it. While his attitude really pissed me off, it turned out for the good, because two weeks later I found a car at a local dealership that was exactly what I'd been looking for all along.

Someone had just traded it in on a new model and the dealership hadn't even had time to get it cleaned up. By happenstance, I spotted it one night when I was heading out for an evening of swilling beer and cruising around and listening to the radio until the wee hours of the morning. The dealership was already closed and the entranceway was blocked, but I stopped anyway and looked at it from afar. I could tell it was a Pontiac Le Mans, but I wasn't certain what model year it was. The Le Mans was Ivy Green with a black vinyl top. The more I stood and looked at it, the more captivated I became. I couldn't just get back in my daddy's Tempest and wait until tomorrow because it was love at first sight. I stepped over the chain and walked to the back of the lot so I could get a closer look, caressing the black vinyl top and exchanging vows of affection with it. Luckily, the doors weren't locked and I was able to open the driver's door and take a seat. Any second an alarm could go off and the police might arrive, but at that moment I couldn't help myself. I had to get behind the wheel.

The next morning, my dad and I rode to the dealership. I could tell he didn't really want me to buy any car sight unseen from a place where he didn't know anybody or had never done business before. I kept my mouth shut and didn't let him know that the only reason he was coming with me was to provide transportation to the lot so I could buy my dream car. He was probably right to be concerned because I have to admit that I paid too much for the car. I basically just took out my checkbook and asked how much? My dad got that disgusted look in his eyes and bit his tongue to keep from telling me what a fool I was. Still, there was little he could say because I was paying for the car with my own money and wasn't asking for a penny from him. This was in direct contrast with the actions of my older brother a few years back, who'd drugged, caroused, and completely wrecked my parents' household finances in his wake, and my dad had footed the bill for all that tomfoolery. Now here he was on the other side of the bargain, with a son who asked only for a ride and was more than willing to do everything else on his own.

After I called the insurance office and had the Le Mans put in my name, I drove to a Shoney's and backed into a stall, ordering myself a Big Boy and onion rings and a small lemonade. I spent the next two hours reading the manual and pre-setting the radio to all my favorite stations. The more time I spent with the Le Mans, the more I became convinced I was experiencing the beginning of a beautiful relationship.

Throughout the summer the Le Mans and I fell more deeply in love. By the time registration for classes came around in September, I was still inventing reasons to be in the Le Mans, driving down every road I could find. I pulled into the school's lot and parked where everyone could see it. Girls were already on campus walking around in the golden post-Labor-Day sunshine. I was happy to be back in college.

For two years, I had been trying to win the affection of a girl who lived off campus in a ritzy neighborhood south of Nashville. I'd worked my way into her sphere of influence through sheer diligence and perseverance, a feat that was never easy considering my lesser economic and social status. Her family consisted of white-collar attorneys and financial consultants, while mine was strictly working class. She lived in a neighborhood where disheveled and rickety Chevys weren't in the habit of pulling into driveways and picking up one of their entitled daughters. I hoped my new shiny and sporty Le Mans would add some prestige to my appearance when I went to see the King's Daughter.

I had a date with her on an October Saturday to go to a movie and maybe eat a pizza afterwards, at which time I would struggle to be entertaining and make her laugh and perhaps forget that I was nothing but a wild boy from the poor side of town and how generally the impoverished like me weren't in this sort of game for the long run and would have to finally drop out of the competition for lack of fundamental assets somewhere along the way. As I drove to her house, I passed by my school and all at once thought of a certain Margaret who lived in one of the dorms, a long tender blonde with blue eyes and a laugh that drew me in every time I heard it. This Margaret was in my 18th Century Lit class, and I sat beside her in those hours learning of Jonathan Swift and Gulliver and looking at her legs crossed there before me, and after a few classes I got brave and invited her to the student center afterwards for a cold drink or coffee. She told me right off the bat she was engaged to a boy back in her hometown of Birmingham, but I chose not to heed the warning, because I was here and he was there, and found I couldn't stop myself from drawing closer to her legs and her eyes and her smile, no matter how dangerous the entire proposition seemed.

That's what was in my mind that Saturday as I pulled through the school gates and parked at the girls' dorm. I'd just finished listening to the Beatles on my 8-track player—the third 8-track player I'd owned since I got the Le Mans two months before—and the lyrics of "Hello, Goodbye" were still playing in my head when I walked into the lobby. I'd forgotten all about my date with the other wealthy out-of-my-league girl I'd invested so much time and money in so far, for now all that was important was to ask for Margaret at the desk—if she hadn't gone home for the weekend—and see her walk down the stairs in all her loveliness. If that came to be, if I heard her laugh and saw her smile and knew it was all for me and not some far-off beau, then I and my sleek and classy Le Mans would be happy for at least one wonderful night never to be forgotten. Who knows, I thought? Maybe I might die in a car accident on the way home, and at least this way I could go to my grave knowing I had spent the last night of my life in the presence of the most beautiful girl in the world and driving home in my classy Le Mans, whether she was technically mine or not and whether the Le Mans was truly the slickest car out there on the road.

All went according to plan for a time. Margaret was indeed in the dorm and bored to death this Saturday, so I forsook the Southern aristocracy of the city and instead vested all my interest in this vision from Alabama. I talked her into going out for a pizza, and she left me there in the lobby to go and get a sweater and her purse. I stood among the chairs and the divans and coffee tables and wondered if this was the night when my ship would come in and my dreams would come true. I thought about how if I could be any happier, I'd probably have no choice but to go on and croak and then ascend to heaven. I hadn't had too tragic of a life so far, but I'd never been this close to paradise either.

We walked among singing birds and chattering squirrels and the golden setting Indian Summer sun to the Le Mans, with its grill smiling at me, its red-line tires glossy black, the ivy green body gleaming and shining brightly. I opened the passenger door for Margaret to get in, and we both stopped then and looked at a conglomeration of twisted wires and ripped upholstery in the floorboard where my fourth 8-track player had been located only a few minutes before. There were oil and dirty fingerprints on the console and the dashboard, and someone had left a rusty screwdriver in the passenger bucket seat.

"Sorry," I told her. "It looks like somebody's stolen my 8-track player."

"That's awful," she said.

"I'm getting used to it," I said.

*****

We never did go eat pizza that night. I had to call the police for insurance purposes and Margaret stood around and waited with me for an hour or so. We talked about school and my four stolen 8-track players and how her boyfriend in Alabama had a Corvette with an anti-theft system in it, and when the cops finally arrived, she said good night and walked by herself back to her dorm. I guess I could have gone back after the cops were gone and to see if she still wanted to go out, but my heart wasn't in it. I kept thinking about her being used to Corvettes and then having to sit in my Le Mans with dirt and grease and leftover fingerprints all around her with no way for me to play "Magical Mystery Tour" or any music whatsoever, since the thief had taken all my tapes too.

I wasn't all that bright, but I knew when I was beaten.

I didn't go see the King's daughter that night either. I just drove home and watched TV until I fell asleep. I waited a few days and called the princess up and told her how sorry I was for standing her up on Saturday night. I told her my aunt died and somebody stole my car. I thought I'd give her a choice of alibis, but I don't know if she believed either one of them.

So, I lost out with her, and Margaret left school at the Christmas break to go home and get married.

The Le Mans and I were facing our last semester of college, alone and on our own. All we had was each other.

I was learning that's just the way it goes sometimes.

9   From Beatlemania to Wildfire on I-40

Tom Nahay

MY FIRST CAR WAS a 1956 Volkswagen Bug. It had a cloth pull-back sun roof, no gas gauge, and a reserve gas tank activated by a toggle bar down by the foot controls. When the car ran out of gas, I simply toggled the bar over to the right and another half a gallon of gas was available. The car had about 30,000 miles on it, needed tires, and had been wrecked on the driver's door and poorly repaired. The car would barely get out of its own way and I was certain the engine was in the throes of death.

How did I come to own such a beauty? I went to work in a neighborhood grocery as a bag boy in 1965. I would go to work when I got out of school, working from 3:00 to 9:00 p.m. Mondays through Fridays and from 11:30–9:00 p.m. on Saturdays, just under 40 hours per week so the owner wouldn't have to pay unemployment tax on me. Previously, I had worked summer jobs cutting yards and painting my grandfather's rental houses in the stifling Southern summer heat and humidity. Since my father had to pick me up at 9:00 every night, he soon tired of this chore because he went to bed with the chickens, given that his job required him to rise early each morning. As a result, it didn't take long before my parents allowed me to buy a VW Beetle that would barely run. Of course, I knew I couldn't expect much for the $160 I paid for it. I also quickly realized that no matter what shape it was in, a ride was still a ride and the VW was my ticket to freedom.

Under the backseat I found the battery compartment and an owner's pamphlet. The engine was located under the rear hatch, and under the front hood was a small trunk and the gas tank. I read the owner's pamphlet and learned that the solid lifters in the little engine's valve train had to be adjusted every 25,000 miles, the oil changed every 3,000 miles, and new spark plugs and points installed every 12,000 miles. Being somewhat mechanically inclined after working with my dad on his cars over the years, I faithfully performed the needed maintenance on my VW Bug and soon had it running like a top. This freed my dad from picking me up every night, so he was happy, which meant my mom was happy. It was a win-win situation all around. The only downside of my new ticket to freedom was that for some reason, car ownership unleashed a wild spirit in me that would guide my actions and thoughts for the next 30 years.

My little VW had a great AM radio that on a clear night, would pick up WLS in Chicago as well as stations in Birmingham. It also had a tiny speaker that I couldn't hear if the windows were rolled down or the top open. It looked small and insignificant parked next to the other kids' cars. Many of them had cars their parents bought for them, and most were great American muscle cars or in some cases, hand-me-down family cars. NO ONE had a Volkswagen. While I was grateful to have a means of transportation, I have to admit that I was envious of those muscle cars with their throaty sounding V-8 engines. However, even my bug turned out to have a bit of a silver lining. I found out soon enough that some of the girls in school who were not so concerned with looking cool and more interested in going places found the VW just fine. An added bonus on date-night was if I rolled back and opened the canvas sunroof, the windows would not steam up while we were making out. I liked that feature. My social life improved a great deal. I even briefly dated my next-door neighbor's sister who lived across town and was a year older than I. To me, she looked a lot like Ann-Margret, so much so that my head would start buzzing when I was around her, trying to make small talk and doing my best not to be dull and boring. Sadly, we didn't date very long, but in a way that was good, because I didn't have to worry anymore about what her sister, my neighbor, was thinking about what was going on while we were out on a date.

Although the Bug needed a set of tires when I got it, dating and drinking beer with my buddies were more important to me, so I put off buying them. Then one rainy day after I gave a girl a ride home, I reached a stop sign but couldn't quite stop. My intention was to go through the stop sign, make a right-hand turn, head down the hill, and drive on to work. When I made the right turn, I hit wet gravel and my bald front tires, having little to no traction, rolled into a lady's mailbox which was mounted on a wrought iron post. The VW was so light in the front with the engine being located in the back, that the iron mailbox lifted the front of the car and the Bug was impaled on a wrought iron post. The post ripped through the floor of the car and into the back of the driver's seat. As the car's momentum carried it forward, the post tore a ten-inch gash in the steel floor of the car. There I was, stuck on a post with no other choice but to call my dad. Needless to say, I feared the worst, especially from my father. I called home and my mother said he wasn't home yet from work. I told her what happened and she asked me if I was hurt. I told her not yet, thinking about what my dad's reaction would be. When he finally arrived, he didn't say much. He talked with the homeowner, who agreed to his plan. He had brought some tools and we jacked up the front of the car, cut off the iron post with a hacksaw, withdrew the post through the sun roof, and freed the car. I started it and backed away from the scene of the crime. The VW had a torn driver's seat and a large hole in the rear floor, but nothing else seemed to be much out of order. My Dad told me to go to work and to tell my boss I would only be working half a day Saturday and that we would discuss the incident later at home. I did as I was instructed, filled with dread about what "later" might mean. The conversation we had turned out to be a learning opportunity for me and also established a standard for parenting that I used later in life. He asked me if I realized how close I had come to being killed. I hadn't thought about that aspect much, so we went out and looked at my wounded Bug. We talked about why it happened, bald tires and speed, and what we were going to do to prevent such a thing from reoccurring. He told me to go see a friend of his who ran a salvage warehouse and find some new tires (I could pay him back later), and he told me to slow down and quit running stop signs. What I had dreaded had not happened. An important lesson from a wise man was gifted to me, a lesson I would use over and over again with my own children. I got the new tires and moved on, even if a bit more carefully, to new heights of teenage dating and carousing with my friends.

The VW served me well until the summer of 1967. I sold it despite my parents' objections and bought a '55 Chevy two-door with a big V-8 engine. My Dad hated the car from the minute I brought it home. He wouldn't even ride in it. By that time, I had been promoted to the meat market of the grocery store and had become a proficient butcher, running the day-to-day operation of the meat market on my own. I even took a second job as a butcher at a big new Giant Foods store across town that had just opened. I worked there from 10:00 p.m. to 3:00 a.m. Monday through Friday and poured every spare dollar into that old Chevy. School, which by now I really hated, was put on the back burner and I was surviving academically by the skin of my teeth. One cold winter's night I came home after work at my usual time and parked my Chevy in the driveway. My Dad had to be at work at 6:00 a.m. and as he was leaving, he didn't see my car in the driveway. He came back in and shook me awake, asking me where I had left my car last night. When I told him I had left it in the driveway, he smiled and replied, "It looks like some of your friends have stolen your car." He loved delivering that news because he had always hated the Chevy. We filed the police report and after a week or so, my dad arranged for me to purchase a car from a friend he worked with for $250. It was a 1961 Mercury Comet two-door, not the cool Comet Caliente with the big V-8 engine but the tamer model with a six-cylinder engine that was grossly underpowered. My dad and I switched emotional roles because now, I was the one who hated that Comet. On a night of drunken revelry one of my friends got sick and vomited in the back floorboard. Thereafter, the car was forever known not as the Comet, but as the "Vomit."

Because my dad seemed so happy that my '55 Chevy had been stolen, I wondered on occasion if perhaps, he had something to do with its disappearance. It was found a month or so later, stripped of its wheels, interior, engine, and transmission, little more than an empty hull dumped into the Cumberland River off the old McGavock Pike Ferry Ramp. The "Vomit" was such a sorry excuse for a car, it made me wish I had my old VW back. Your first car is like your first love, the one you never forget. Still, as they say in show business, "the show must go on."

It was late fall of 1968. It had been a record-setting hot summer in the South and everything was dry as a bone. The draft for the Vietnam War was in progress, but the lottery system had been not yet been implemented. I did not try to go to college because as I stated previously, my abhorrence of high school had left me academically marooned with grades so bad that no school would accept me. I felt as if I had a target on my back, inviting the Federal Government to come get me, which indeed I did, because I had no draft deferment. My expectation was that I would be drafted, trained in the rudiments of being a soldier, and then sent to be killed in some nameless rice paddy in Southeast Asia.

In the midst of all this, I decided to make a last-ditch effort to reunite with my first love before going off to the war in Southeast Asia. I had been going on and off with a girl I grew up with. I had known her since second grade and we had always been close friends. We really started dating regularly by the 11th grade, but would break up, then get back together again, and on and on it went. I started to become very serious about her in the summer of 1968. I bought a ring and popped the question right after graduation. When she said, "yes," I was elated. I got a marriage license that summer and rented a house for us to live in when we got married in the fall. She was a really sweet girl, but her dad and older brother did NOT like me one bit. Maybe in her father's judgement, given that I wasn't attending college and was working a nowhere job, I was more suited for the draft than marriage to his daughter. He finally was able to pressure her into saying "no" to my proposal, maybe even to prevent her from becoming a wartime widow. His way of thinking makes some kind of sense to me now, but certainly not then. Regardless, in a short time she tearfully gave me the engagement ring back, saying she just couldn't go through with it because she wasn't sure she loved me "like that." She went off to college in the fall, but when she came home to visit, she would always let me know in advance and we would go out. This scrambled my emotions and brain even more, making me think I still had a chance to win her back.

The college she attended was in a small town where the school was the center of both town and campus life. It was a long drive from where I lived and an even longer drive into the dreamworld I was trying to create in my mind. I had a nice '63 Chevy Impala with a high output small V-8 I had done a lot of work on, and it ran to perfection. I headed out I-40 West one morning to visit what I still my hoped would be my future wife. Our weekend went well. I didn't mention commitment or anything like that and neither did she. We didn't speak the "L" word like we used to do, didn't talk about future plans, or the War, or what I was going to do to not get killed in Vietnam. We just kept it light. When it came time to leave late that Sunday afternoon for the long drive back home, we kissed and she cried because she said we could never be together. My emotions were exploding like solar flares and felt like shrapnel wounds in my heart and head. By the time I turned onto the entry ramp for I-40 East, it was getting late and the sun was going down behind me. I had this sick feeling that the sun was also going down on our relationship, or more correctly, the relationship we had once had. I traveled about 40 miles up the interstate, pushing the Chevy hard when my right rear tire suddenly blew out. I managed to pull safely to the shoulder of the road. Retrieving the bumper jack and the spare tire and lug wrench from the trunk, I started changing the flat tire. On that particular day, traffic on I-40 was extremely heavy, especially with semi-trucks. The wind from every semi that passed by shook the Chevy. By the time I had the car jacked up, it was pitch-dark and the only way I could see was from the headlights of the passing vehicles. I had no flashlight and had already removed all the lug nuts from the wheel of the flat tire, and had placed them in the baby moon hubcap I had set down beside the car so I wouldn't lose them. When I removed the wheel of the flat tire, I leaned it against the rear fender. As I put the spare on the car, a semi-truck passed by too closely and the wind from its passing shook the car, knocking over the wheel of the flat tire. Like dominos, the wheel of the flat tire fell over hitting the hubcap that contained the lug nuts, flipping the lug nuts out into the dry weeds along the roadside and into the darkness. The lug nuts were lost, but I knew I had to find them because I didn't have money to call a wrecker. This was long before cell phones existed so I would have to walk God only knew how far to get help. I began looking around for something, anything in the car, that would help me find the missing lug nuts. I saw some old newspapers lying in the trunk and grabbing them up, twisted them into a long bundle. My bright idea was if I could light them with my cigarette lighter, I might be able to create a makeshift torch to help me find the lost lug nuts.

I lit the paper torch and began to search the weeded area. I found three of the lug nuts and knew they would be enough to get the spare on and make it home. As I was screwing the lug nuts onto the wheel studs, the torch burned down close to my hand so I tossed it away. When I finally finished tightening the lug nuts and looked behind me, the dry grass on the shoulder of the road was burning. The wind caused by passing traffic rapidly fanned it into a raging brush fire. The fire was already too big for me to put out. All I could do was leave and try to get help. I peeled out of there and drove up I-40 East, punching that Chevy's V-8 for all it was worth. I had every intention of stopping at the next exit and reporting the fire. Then I noticed a State Trooper and a fire truck headed back on I-40 West toward the fire with emergency lights flashing and sirens blaring. I thought to myself, *this can't be good.* Now even more freaked out, I kept driving east. I could see the huge brush fire and flashing lights of the emergency vehicles in my rear-view mirror as I sped toward home, still hours away. I knew that going back to help with the fire was probably the right thing to do. I also knew it would most likely get me into deep trouble. Even though my conscience bothered me, I kept punching the Impala, driving away from the fire toward the safety of home.

The next day I overheard my parents talking to each other about the local news report of a huge brush fire on I-40 East that had closed the two lanes on the Interstate for several hours. I hid behind my best poker face and said I wondered how such a thing like that could have happened. I said nothing else about the ill-fated fire or my broken heart.

There may be a statute of limitations for everything. In time, I did get over the fire and the girl, and my broken heart, and somehow survived the draft of 1968.

10 The Car Makes the Man

Bob Dietz

IT WASN'T MY CAR. And I never drove it. But it may have set me on a life path as assuredly as stepping into one of the cars at Knoebels Park's giant wooden roller coaster guaranteed you a rocket ride from Point A to Point B.

It was a 1974 Lincoln Town Car, and the owner was Danny, my friend who lived a block away in our little coal mining town, population 6,000. Danny and I had graduated from high school in the spring, and we both had turned 18, just in time for the 1975 football season. I date the Lincoln in those terms, not because Danny had been an All-Conference defensive end, but because it's the axis on which my relationship with the Lincoln was impaled, because sometimes small, brief experiences can set you on a course as inflexible as lane three on a high-school track.

Danny had called to ask if I wanted to take a ride in his new car. I said, "sure." When I walked out of my house and headed to Danny's place, my eyes caught sight of a dark blue gleaming monstrosity parked in the middle of the next block. A new Lincoln in our neighborhood looked as out of place as actor Pauly Shore's bombshell dates sharing his Kodak moments. Danny and I both lived "on the wrong side of the tracks," as evidenced by the railroad tracks that were less than a hundred yards to our west, and our street was named Railroad Avenue. Lincolns did not belong on Railroad Avenue.

As I approached, the magnificent vehicle came into full view. Waves of questions came to mind regarding its origins, the limitless potentialities of whoever owned it, and—wait a minute—surely this could not be Danny's "new car"! The Lincoln sat there, a few feet from Danny's front step. Could it be? I stopped and thought about Danny for a moment. He was a 6'3" better-looking version of Fonzie. A guy who, when he was 15, hung out with 20-somethings most of the time. When a group of us 15-year-olds were stopped by the cops for violating curfew and Danny was with us, the police would address Danny with, "Now you'll be sure to get these boys home, right?" Danny would answer "oh yeah," and all would be right with the world. I don't know how old the cops thought Danny was, but it wasn't 15.

Standing a few feet from the Lincoln, I suddenly realized that there was a very good chance that, God knows how, it might indeed be Danny's new car. There was certainly an otherworldliness to the Town Car being parked here on Railroad Avenue, but also a kind of resonance, as if a glowing hot meteorite had smacked down into one of the strip mine craters a hundred yards away. The meteorite may not belong anywhere on earth, but a strip mine crater is at least--karmically speaking--a good home for it. Maybe the Lincoln had somehow found its way here, to the one spot on Railroad Avenue where it might in fact belong.

The front door of Danny's house opened. "So what do you think?" he asked, with a hint of a smile.

The only car I had driven much to that point was my green 1970 Dodge Dart, a hand-me-down from my father. The Dart had decent power, decent handling, and never failed to start on a frigid 10-degree morning. The best car in which I had regularly ridden was my friend Mark's classy Ford Elite, a lovely vehicle bought at auction.

That first time I slid into the passenger seat of Danny's Lincoln, however, I knew that I was in something completely different from those other vehicles, something completely alien to what I was familiar with. For starters, the Lincoln smelled new. Not car-wash-deodorizer new, but clean and fresh and with the subtle fragrance of a new leather jacket. Amazingly, every time I was in that car, it smelled just as new.

The seats were black leather, supple but firm and supportive. My 140-pound frame was indeed "seated" properly every time I lowered myself into place. The biggest surprise was that the Lincoln had electric seat controls. To me, these seat controls were something straight out of *Star Trek*. All of my father's vehicles had manual windows and manual seat adjustment. The Lincoln had electric windows, but it was the electric seats that really placed me in an altered passenger state of mind.

Pressing buttons that resulted in a car seat quietly whirring me this way and that for optimal comfort was a completely novel and pampered experience. Steady, efficient movements, with me simply pressing buttons, tilting me forward and back or sliding me closer to the dash or farther away. I was used to shoving levers and planting my feet and jerking seats forward and back in uncontrolled clumsy spasms. These electric seats were utterly different, and the ambience they created in the Lincoln's elegant interior was totally new.

The Lincoln accelerated smoothly, but weighing close to 5,500 pounds, it took about 12 seconds for it to get up to speed. Once it got rolling, handling on the winding state roads of Schuylkill County figured to be a problem. With Danny behind the wheel, however, there were no issues. Electric windows humming up and down. Electric seats positioning us perfectly. The car itself was beautifully insulated from outside sounds. The entire experience was seamless, and that included the driver.

Danny, you see, was not a guy who moved in spurts, fast then slow, clumsily shoving his body through space. He always had a steady, measured flow to him. He moved like David Carradine in the old *Kung Fu* television series. Unhurried, purposeful, never anxious or caught by surprise, he moved in the same manner as the electric windows and seats, and the smooth acceleration of the Lincoln itself. And Danny spoke the same way that he moved. Clear of tone, but never emotional or hurried, he always seemed to be one step ahead of whatever was going on. Being in that Lincoln with Danny driving, was all of a piece.

That first ride in the Town Car was on a Tuesday. Danny drove me to Shamokin, about 20 miles from our hometown. We were going to a place called The Jester Club to meet the people from whom Danny had bought his new car. It didn't occur to me to ask how he could afford the Lincoln. I figured if he wanted me to know, he'd tell me.

When we arrived at the huge standalone building, the nightclub was closed, but Danny knocked and in we went. He introduced me to the guys who owned and ran the place. I didn't realize it at the time, but they had probably told Danny to bring anyone who might be assisting him in his errands so they could give them the once-over. I had a little bit of a profile in the local area, having graduated first in my high school class and snagging my high school's first National Merit Scholarship. I was a bad boy anomaly, I suppose, but The Jester Club evidently gave me the thumbs up because I accompanied Danny on many errands in the weeks and months ahead.

All of those errands included us in the Lincoln. Most of them involved driving through Schuylkill and adjoining counties and picking up money from the previous week's sports betting losers and paying the previous week's winners. We did most of this at night, and we had to ensure that we weren't followed or didn't run into any major problems.

Most of the pick-ups and drop-offs involved amounts ranging from $1,000 to $5,000. Occasionally a single transaction could be in the $15,000 range, so Danny was carrying a fair amount of cash on him most of the time, especially if it was a night with multiple stops. Our protocols were simple. Sitting in the back seat, I had a little wire ring notepad containing the sports teams and amounts for each bettor. Danny would ease the Lincoln into some parking lot somewhere, and we would do a *Miami Vice* type of meetup. The other vehicle arrived, and the bettor got out of his car and slid into the front passenger seat of the Lincoln. Danny would explain the count and amount and then either collect or pay. If there was a discrepancy, I was called upon to state the teams, spreads, and financial tally for each. Since I had a good memory for numbers, once I had read the notepad page, I could rattle everything off the top of my head. People sometimes found that impressive, which amused us.

The Lincoln was the centerpiece that made it all work. My take was that most of the bettors had no idea that The Jester Club was running things. They thought Danny and "the math guy" were the bookmakers. Anyone owning the Lincoln was assumed to be the person in charge. Cash transactions of $15,000 in the Town Car's front seat seemed no more out of place than at the local bank. The Town Car's ambience granted us the required gravitas. Danny always moved and spoke with his defensive-end, David-Carradine style, and I just sat in the back seat rattling off numbers like the Kingpin's accountant. I never addressed any of the bettors by name, and I never said "Danny." Real names weren't even allowed in the notepad. The Lincoln was a tight ship.

We were a couple of barely 18-year-olds cruising around with bags of cash, calmly doing our job for The Jester Club. I have no idea if some of the gamblers went home thinking, *that accountant in the back seat looks young* or what, but we always pulled it off. The Lincoln was our magic wand. We never encountered a real problem. Once in a while, a bettor would be short of cash, usually after a particularly bad five-figure week. Danny would then respectfully and quietly utter his go-to line, "That's unacceptable," and he'd tell the person that we'd be in touch. Then Danny would drive back to The Jester Club and they would say they'd take care of it. The following week the money was always right.

On two occasions, the folks running The Jester Club tested us. We returned to the club after an evening of errands, and they said that the amount we had given them was short by three or four grand. They would run down the games and figures, Danny would turn to me, and without resorting to notes, I would explain that the Minnesota in their listing was the college Gophers, not the NFL Vikings, and that was their error. Each time, they immediately agreed, and it was pretty clear that they were just yanking our chain to see how we'd respond. Danny always handled these moments with aplomb. I wasn't stressed because ripping them off or being anything but completely honest with them never entered my mind.

I ran errands in the Lincoln with Danny until the end of the 1976 football season, when I headed off to Penn State's main campus. At no time had I ever taken a beverage of any kind into the Town Car. The thought of something syrupy dribbling into the cup holders was sacrilegious. And an errant French fry never wound up on the Lincoln's floor mats. The Lincoln was not that kind of car. There were no drunken joyrides or women who entered the *sanctum sanctorum*.

It was a sacred place. In that car, I was treated as a respected adult even though I was doing questionable things, as adults occasionally do. Those electric seats and that subtle leather smell defined the chapel in which I slowly transitioned into adulthood. Gravitas seeped from every pore of that car, and I was fortunate enough to absorb a bit of it.

Shortly after I left for Penn State, I heard that the guys at The Jester Club had finally tracked down a pink slip for Danny to attach to the Lincoln. I guess it was about time.

I miss that car and those adventures more with each passing day. Danny wound up owning a title company in Manhattan and was very successful. He took his employees on annual trips to Las Vegas, where they stayed at either Mandalay Bay or downtown at The Golden Nugget. He eventually sold his company and retired. I never asked Danny what happened to the Lincoln, probably because I didn't want to know. I didn't want to hear that it had been sold or traded in or simply retired due to the ravages of miles and wear. I prefer to think of it still out there on those nighttime county roads, stopping and picking up payments during each week of football season. Perhaps *sans* driver, a kind of Town Car version of Christine from the Stephen King novel. I might age and wither, but not that Lincoln.

As for me, Danny and that car set me on an unusual path that I have never regretted. I've been a professional sports bettor for 45 years. Odds are, I owe all of it to the Lincoln.

11 My Foreign Affairs

Ralph Bland

WHETHER IT CONCERNED WOMEN or automobiles, I have always been a sucker for a pretty face. As with a beautiful girl, in the past I have invested my all and everything into those smiling grills and sleek features. On more than one occasion, I have fooled myself into thinking that by owning such a vehicle life would be rosy and glorious, especially when experienced from behind the wheel of a two-seater convertible from across the Atlantic. This kind of attitude has cost me a great deal of money through the years. I have also suffered moments of pain and angst while standing along the side of a road with the hood raised, waiting for assistance and wondering if a tow truck would arrive before criminals or joyriding hoodlums caught sight of me.

Yes, sports cars have always been like women to my way of thinking. They torture and tease. They can bring me to the point of tears, causing me at times to stand on the high cliffs of the old psyche and look down into the abyss and wonder if this might be the proper time to take the quick easy whoopsie-doo off the edge. And where sports cars are concerned, put an end to all the chaos and suffering brought on by a conglomeration of overseas metal. Yet, like some women I have known, cars also have—along with their moments of woe—times of uncontrollable joy.

On the first of this month, I marked another anniversary with Zelda, my 1971 MGB. This milestone has given me pause to reflect

on the long litany of British sports cars that spans almost five de-
cades of my foreign car affairs.

SALLY

My first foray into British sports car ownership came in the
mid-1970s when I bought something called a Sunbeam Tiger
off, ironically, a Sunbeam bread vendor. The Tiger was red with
spoked wheels and almost ten years old. The only time I had seen a
Sunbeam Tiger before was while watching *Get Smart* on television
and seeing Elizabeth Taylor wrap one around a tree in *Butterfield
8*. I named the Sunbeam Sally because she had a nice smile. For
the next several years, Sally and I roared around Nashville and out
into the countryside on wild late-night rides into the wee small
hours of the morning. When I say "roar" I really mean it. Sally
was equipped with an engine the size of a small jet-liner and with
the slightest press of the accelerator liked to take flight. Being that
I was young enough to be a bit of a lunatic, taking my life into
my hands each time I got behind the wheel seemed to have some
sort of twisted, fantastic appeal. I can remember driving Sally to
Pensacola for a week of hedonistic fun and watching in fascination
as the speedometer passed 140 mph. With the top down and the
frame shimming and shaking, I wondered if I had enough guts
enough to try steering Sally with my toes.

It was not pretty.

This is probably the abiding reason God chose to have Sally
explode in my workplace parking lot one afternoon. A blown gas-
ket and cracked block required a host of mechanical setbacks only
a millionaire could afford to fix. My co-workers at the time were
so moved by my loss that they went to a nearby cemetery and ap-
propriated flowers and wreaths from a recent funeral and taking
an 8' by 10' photograph for posterity's sake, cloaked a *Rest in Peace*
banner over what was left of Sally. That picture still sits on my
desk looking at me while I work. It is like the picture of the dead
wife in the novel *Rebecca*, a reminder of love gone terribly wrong.
The truth is Sally was taken from me by a benevolent Maker who

wanted to save me from self-destruction. Still, there will always be a part of me that will never stop loving her.

ELIZABETH

Elizabeth was a British Racing Green 1979 MGB, whom I bought brand spanking new from a high-end dealership in downtown Nashville. She was all I dreamed of for a couple of months, until the afternoon a lady ran into the back of us at a four-way stop sign, crushing Elizabeth's trunk and damaging the fuel cut-off control. After that mishap, no matter how many times she was supposedly repaired, Elizabeth never performed completely up to par again. I learned for the first time how this sort of behavior was one of those British car things, one of those mysterious mechanical phenomena that couldn't be understood or fixed by any mechanic. Unfortunately, it was a lesson I would frequently have to re-learn. In time, I came to accept that I would have to live with what became a continuing string of maladies.

Elizabeth would run fine for periods of time, then out of nowhere come to a petulant halt and stop with no warning. She often toyed with me, stranding me in rush hour traffic, in distant parking lots, in Timbuctoo, and other unnamed destinations. Sometimes, I would stand in front of Elizabeth and make threats or plead with her. When that didn't work, I learned always to take a book along with me so I would have something to do until she decided to start up again, which she would often do for no reason at all other than she wanted to.

Once, I made a big play for a particular lady of interest. I took her out for dinner and a movie on a hot, July night. When we came out of the movie, we decided to take a nice leisurely drive beneath a luminous summer moon. We traveled about fifty yards before Elizabeth sighed, gasped and whispered, "See you later." It was eleven o'clock at night and the woman I had tried so hard to impress had to help me push Elizabeth up a small rise to get her into a vacant parking lot. The pre-cellphone days meant that I had to leave the woman alone with Elizabeth and trek to a distant phone booth to call one of my grinning friends to come and please pick us up. Needless to say, my grand romantic gesture did not end well. It was a clear "thumbs down" as far as my date was concerned. Apparently, she was not the least bit adventurous and had no sense of humor about being stranded at a deserted shopping mall when it was approaching midnight.

Elizabeth's time with me ended when a tree fell on her on a calm summer morning while she was parked in my driveway. The sun was shining and there was not even a trace of breeze when a huge limb fell and crushed her convertible top into particles resembling Chicklets. I knew I was beaten. It was time for goodbyes. I traded her in for a pickup truck later that afternoon.

MARTHA

I have heard it said that time heals all wounds. Maybe that's why I waited almost a decade before I got back into another foreign affair. I saw a shiny 1973 red roadster sitting in someone's front yard with a For Sale sign in the window. I kept driving by the house for the rest of the week until I finally stopped and rang the doorbell.

The fellow who owned her was nobody's fool. He took my first offer.

Martha was fine for a while, but she proved soon enough that she was not one to be trusted. It was not entirely her fault and it was true that I had been burned before by her ilk, so I did my best to make certain I always had a second car available—a real car, loyal, faithful, and reliable. I was determined not to fall prey to any British shenanigans again.

On a snowy night I got off work late and started up Martha to head home. When my left foot pushed to the floorboard with no resistance, I knew the clutch was gone. Naturally there had been no warning. It was as if Martha had waited until I worked past closing and everyone had gone home, not to mention icy snow falling like runaway dandruff. I had no choice but to walk the two miles home and leave her sitting alone, exposed to the elements.

The next day I learned that in order to replace Martha's clutch, the engine had to be pulled. What a surprise. I had never heard of anything like that before. When I learned how much replacing said clutch would run me, I thanked God I had no children to support, no college tuition to pay off, and didn't have to shell out alimony for an ex-spouse. I had to work a lot of overtime to make enough money to get her fixed and running again. After two months in a mechanic's garage, I got Martha back and drove her to work. I parked on a slight incline, put the gearshift in first and pulled up the hand brake. After I had taken about ten steps away, I heard a clicking sound and turned to see Martha slowly rolling away, picking up speed as she headed through the parking lot toward a road that spilled out into a busy suburban street. I tried to catch her, but I was too slow.

She didn't make it to the bottom of the hill and into the street. Instead, she decided to veer off to her left and clip a couple of parked cars before running into a bascart retrieval corral. Although I had insurance, I said a few words to Martha in the heat of the moment that day that could never be taken back.

I'd grown smarter over the years. I put dear Martha up for sale.

I took the first offer.

EMILY

Twenty years passed before I considered owning another British sports car. I retired in 2012, and one of the first things I did was start behaving like the idiot from my former youth. Although I should have known better, I was determined I wouldn't be made a fool of again by a pretty face. This time I would cast my lot in the romantic wars of two-seaters with a different car from another country. There would be no further British automotive temptations in my life.

Then I came across Emily.

She was shiny black with polished spoke wheels and an impeccable body. "Take her for a drive if you'd like," the seller said.

So I cruised through the suburban neighborhood of Spring Hill, Tennessee, wandering out on I-65. I watched the needle rise effortlessly to 70 mph. She was a 1979 MGB, 33 years old at the time and I was 62. Perhaps, she was too young for me, but I figured we'd both been around and that we could be good for each other.

One clear, blue morning the key, for some reason, stuck in the ignition and I had to have Emily towed to a garage. I informed the mechanic that she seemed to be leaking a little oil. Can you fix that too? One thing led to another and it took almost a month before I got the call to come get her. I gave the mechanic my arm and a leg in payment. I even threw in my eye-teeth as a tip. On the way home smoke began rising from the floorboard. I tried at first to ignore it, but it began seeping out from the dashboard to the point where I had difficulty seeing. A car pulled up beside me and a guy yelled out of his window, "Hey, buddy, your car is on fire." Emily left me once again. It seemed obvious enough that our relationship was one of "rinse and repeat."

A few days after Emily finally made it home, I went to meet my wife for dinner. I was singing along with Linda Ronstadt to "You're No Good" on the radio when I noticed a Mercedes pull out of a strip mall. I watched it coming my way, as if in slow motion, figuring sooner or later it would surely stop. And it did stop—when it hit me, obliterating Emily's passenger side and knocking us twenty-odd feet, bending the steering wheel in my hands like I was Superman from Krypton setting down in Music City, USA.

Emily was t-boned. Emily was totaled. She would never be on the road again. I felt that odd pervasive feeling of doom and sadness wash over me while I watched the wrecker haul her away. Goodbye, Emily.

ZELDA

I found Zelda on eBay. She was in Washington state, 2000 miles away. There was a picture and a box to place a bid. I put in a figure and waited a week. Then an email came and said I was the winner.

I named her Zelda after F. Scott Fitzgerald's pretty, schizophrenic wife. I drove her around and waited for her to break down, to blow up, to fall to pieces before my eyes, but nothing happened. Zelda chugged on. On occasion she needed things, a starter, a battery, and a distributor. There were also times when her mystic persona appeared and made itself known, like the way the speedometer stopped working on weekdays and then functioned perfectly on Saturdays and Sundays. Still, over time, I learned to live with her and she learned to live with me. Just don't ask for too much, she told me. I am old. I am 47—that'd 329 in dog years. Ah, Zelda, but I am old too. I have learned to never ask for too much and to be satisfied with very little. And occasionally, when a miracle comes along, to be overwhelmed with gratitude.

And so, we are content, Zelda and I, happy in our limited road trip forays into the outside world.

One other thing.

On a warm September afternoon, I found myself standing at a gas pump, filling Zelda's tank with high test. A beautiful young lady approached me with dark raven hair, smiling blue eyes, cheekbones high and prominent, all the things a young man's dreams are made of.

"My daddy had a car like this," she said, running her finger across Zelda's green fender. "He used to take me for rides in it when I was a little girl. He'd always put the top down and the wind would blow through my hair. I just love cars like this!"

"I do too," was all I managed to say, for I was older and this sort of chance meeting no longer held the allure it once had. But it was nice to remember such encounters were still possible in the world.

I got behind the wheel and turned on the ignition. The motor made a nice purring sound as I drove away, and I knew the pretty girl was standing there at the pumps watching me and Zelda disappear down the road. The top was down and the sun was shining, and another wondrous day was in full swing.

12 Mopar Madness

Alan Longmire

LET'S START BY SAYING I come from long line of Chrysler admirers on my father's side. There are family stories about four generations of Chrysler products, tales of supernatural performance and immortal mechanical ability. There was my great grandfather's 1924 Dodge Brothers touring car (technically not a Chrysler product, but still. . .) that once stalled out while fording a creek in what is now Chuck Swan Wilderness Area east of Sharp's Chapel, a remote and wild section of Union County, Tennessee. Rather than ask my great grandmother to step out of the car and ruin her dress, Grandad Longmire simply put the car in gear and used the electric starter, a novel thing in those days, to crawl the car across the creek and up the bank.

There was my grandfather's 1939 Plymouth Coupe with the venetian blinds in the rear window that he drove while courting the woman who was to become my grandmother. Then there was also the 1952 Plymouth panel truck that valiantly served the grocery store my grandfather (known to us as Paw) started in Corryton, Tennessee, after the War. For a while it pulled double duty, becoming the vehicle my dad and uncle learned to drive on.

A few years later, the legendary 1958 Plymouth Fury came along. My grandfather bought it because he thought an urbane, yet sporty, sophisticate like himself deserved, as he referred to it, "the most powerful car ever built." Just over 5,000 were made, all the same color, dressed out in Buckskin Beige. My grandfather's

Fury came equipped with the Golden Commando package, a 350 cubic inch V-8 with dual Carter AFB four-barrel carburetors and an ungodly amount of horsepower. It became something of a legend within our clan as the result of an incident that occurred in 1959. He drove the family to Kansas City to see where he'd spent a brief part of his youth before the Depression sent him back home to Union County. Somewhere between Columbus, Missouri, and St. Louis, a brand new 1959 Cadillac El Dorado whizzed past him and cut him off. Now, Paw was not a man to take such an insult lightly, so he floored the Fury in pursuit, passed the Caddy, and kept going. My father, then a 12-year-old, kept peeking over the back seat to see how fast they were going, but my grandfather kept swatting him back with a "Siddown, boy, it's dangerous!" Later, while they were parked at a roadside picnic area, a Missouri State Trooper came flying by, then skidded to a stop and backed up, blocking them in. "Do you know how fast you were going?" the trooper asked in a respectful tone. Paw said "Nope. You catch that Cadillac?" The trooper said "Yeah, and I clocked him at 125. You, I'm gonna say were running 150, because I couldn't even gain on you, much less catch you. Take this ticket and get the hell out of my state before I change my mind. And take it easy on that car." I always assumed this was a bit of an exaggeration until the day we were packing up Paw's desk during a move and found the ticket.

Paw sold the Fury before Dad turned 16. He bought himself a 1964 Chrysler Imperial and made Dad drive a '63 Ford Falcon until, as he put it, Dad learned to stay out of the ditches. When Uncle Dale turned 16, Paw bought he and my dad a matched pair of 1966 Dodge Coronet 500 coupes with four-barrel 383's. Dad's car was yellow with an automatic, while Dale's was red and had a four-speed transmission.

My brother came along in 1966, and I followed in 1970. Paw, in the meantime, was the first one in the family to break the Chrysler streak. Since Chrysler had stopped making Imperials in 1965, he decided to buy a 1967 Cadillac because he wanted something classy. Dale kept the Coronet until his hero, Richard Petty, stopped driving Chrysler products and switched to Pontiac. Of course, Dale followed suit. The grocery store's truck continued to be a Chrysler product, a 1967 Dodge with a 12-foot box bed and three on the floor. So that's the backstory. Growing up in such a tradition, I knew when I got my first car, by God, it was going to be a Mopar of some sort, preferably a later 1960s muscle car variety.

In 1977, Dad started his own store, and my brother and I worked there from the day it opened. I was seven, and back then child labor laws didn't apply to family—or so I was told. The two perks of working there were A: we got paid minimum wage, and B: we had free rein to look at all the car magazines. We also were able to ask the magazine guy to stock ALL of them. We took full advantage. My brother being older, got started buying cars first. He went through a Karmann-Ghia convertible that never ran right; a '71 Buick Riviera fastback, ditto; and a '76 Ford Fairlane coupe with a Mustang engine, all by the time he turned 16. The Fairlane got traded for a '79 Formula Firebird. After he totaled the Firebird, he entered into the realm of Mopar once more, buying a sporty little compact, a Plymouth Tourismo 2.2. Over the course of the next year, he brought home a '66 Coronet 500 and a '58 Dodge sedan. This doesn't include the '49 Plymouth sedan he had purchased a couple of years earlier "as a Christmas present for our mother," which of course, didn't fool anyone. By the time I was thirteen, I had my heart set on a 1970 Plymouth Barracuda owned by one of the other Mopar nuts in our community. It had a 340 cubic inch V-8 with three two-barrel carburetors, the famous 340 six-pack, and a Hurst four-speed transmission topped off with a walnut-handled pistol-grip shifter. It was also missing third gear, didn't run, and cost about five times what I could afford. It didn't take long before I started looking further afield.

Keep in mind that at this point, I had memorized every model and option the Chrysler Corporation had produced between about 1958 and 1971 and would have settled for just about anything but a Valiant or a Dart. I actually waffled a bit about the '63-'66 Darts, since they had a cool little forward-sloping notch in the rear side window opening on the two-door sedans. Still, no matter how cool they looked, a Dodge Dart was NOT a cool car, then or ever. Then one day when I was looking through a copy of some sales listings that included cars from all over east Tennessee, I saw it— a 1964 Plymouth Belvedere two-door sedan. Classier than a Dart or Valiant could ever be, but could be bought new with any engine Mopar offered, up to the 426 Max Wedge. Unlike the coupe, it also had that nifty little angle in the back side windows that I was drawn to. Even better, it was $400, which meant I could actually afford it! The only catch was that it was in Ringgold, Georgia, just across the state line from Chattanooga, and being that I had just turned 14, I couldn't go get it anyway.

Luckily, Dad, being a car nut as well, was amenable to helping me out. He and Dale had bought a 1924 Model T Ford when they were 16 and 12 years old and, wonder of wonders, had even tracked down and bought back what was left of Paw's old '58 Fury the year before. Dad was able to talk our milkman into letting us borrow him and his car hauler to go down to Ringgold and get the Belvedere. I spent the whole trip floating above the back seat of that truck. When we arrived at the address, there it was—big, boxy, and beautiful. Sure, it was the color of cat food, and rather than a big V-8, it had the dinky 225 slant six. Still, it did have a 727 Torque-flight, three-speed automatic transmission and the ultra-cool pushbutton automatic option. This meant that rather than a shift lever on the steering column or floor, it had a row of rectangular buttons, running vertically down the left side of the instrument panel. PRND21 never looked so good. Instead of that awkward arm-wrestling motion shifters required, all I had to do was press a button and glide away. And I did, tooling around the block in an attempt to look like I was seriously taking a test drive and might not even buy the thing. "How about power brakes?" "All the power you can stomp 'em with." "Power steering?" "See how big and square the wheel is? That's so it feels like power steering, 'cause you got all that leverage." "Will you take $350?" "$400—take it or leave it." I handed over the money without a second thought, proud that I had at least asked. We loaded it up on the car-hauler trailer and set off back to Knox County. I don't think I ever looked out of the window that whole trip because I was too busy staring at my new obsession.

Now came the planning. My brother and I would have long conversations about how I would fix it up to be the best sleeper hot rod ever seen with no expense spared. We took off the cheap-looking entry-level chrome trim and Bondo-patched the holes. Someone had installed air shocks in the back with a hand-pump mechanism that allowed you to overload the trunk, then pump it back up so it rode level. I later found out that meant it was probably used to run moonshine, which made it even more badass.

It had to have a good engine. After looking at the price of big-block V-8s, I realized there had been a niche market in the 1960's for hot-rodding the venerable 225 slant-six. I found an Offenhauser intake manifold that would allow me to put on a four-barrel carburetor instead of the puny one-barrel it came with. I couldn't afford them or install them, but I knew where they were. The stock exhaust manifold was cracked in two right down the middle, so it sounded pretty mean as it was. I could live with that. Maybe not perfect, but good enough.

Those stock steel wheels had to go. Did I want the American Racing slot mags? Turbines? Baby Moon hubcaps and chrome rims? Nope. Gotta have billet aluminum solid disks. Raise the tail a little, too. Put a sway bar on that puppy and watch it take those corners like the first cousin of Richard Petty's '64 Fury that won every race it was in. Can I afford that? No? Well, I could at least add it to the list.

And the color. "Used brown cat food" is not an exaggeration. Plymouth called it Bronze, but 20 years of weather had left it a dull, muddy brown, a little bit darker than a standard mud puddle. This is where I had my stroke of genius: Use the later 1960's "Scat Pack" colors like "Go Bananas yellow" or "Go Mango orange?" No. It had to be "Plum Crazy," a dark metallic purple that Prince himself would have orgasmed over. And while we are at it, let's add a black stripe around the tail like the later Roadrunner, and hey, isn't the Roadrunner a Belvedere too?

As with all projects, there were setbacks. Money failed to roll in at the pace which I required. I did get the alternator rebuilt when I acquired a girlfriend at the age of 15 in order to drive her up and down the driveway. Having a quarter-mile driveway is great when you can't take it on an actual road. That is, until it dies at the bottom end and won't start. The next day I was riding to the mall with my girlfriend and her mother, talking about the incident when she asked if we had gotten the car back to the house. With the worst Freudian slip ever recorded, I said, "Yeah, we had to jack it off. JUMP! I MEAN JUMP IT OFF! JUMP START! BATTERY! CABLES! I don't know what that other word means, I swear!" The fact that I am still alive is proof that it is not possible for one to die of embarrassment, but all these years later, it still makes me cringe. I don't know how Mrs. Jones kept a straight face OR let me keep dating her daughter.

Now comes the sad part. I was going to turn sixteen in one week. Dad took me out to the Belvedere and said "You gonna drive this thing?" I said, "Yes, of course I will." He pointed to the non-power brakes, the non-power steering. I assured him that I could handle it. He pointed to the bare, solid steel dashboard. I shrugged and replied, "Yeah, so?" He pointed to the lack of seat belts. I suddenly realized where he was headed, and my heart dropped when he said, "If you get in a wreck in this piece of junk, they'll just hose you off the dashboard and sell it to another kid. You're not driving this thing on the road." I spent that next week begging and pleading to no avail. I even ordered seatbelts from the J.C. Whitney catalog. It didn't matter. My brother and grandfather all agreed: The Belvedere was not in any shape to drive on the road. End of argument.

On the morning of my 16th birthday, I felt like crap. Even though we went to Rutledge and got my license, I had no car. After two years of fantasizing and some hard work, I had no car. My dream Belvedere was not to be. On the way home from the DMV, I was still heartbroken. Then Dad said "Hey, you know that '69 T-bird in Mr. Zachary's garage? It has seatbelts and power everything. You can have it if you sell that Belvedere and pay me back." Was I dreaming? Rainbows suddenly appeared in the sky. A shower of hearts and flowers fell from the heavens. I was gonna have wheels! That is how I happened to be a 16-year-old kid in possession of a red 1969 Thunderbird coupe with black leather seats and a stainless interior AND a 426 Cobra-jet engine. To this day, I know I could never thank Dad enough for his miraculous act of generosity.

Still, looking back on the many cars I have bought and the miles I have driven them, when all is said and done, I still miss that Belvedere the most.

13 Automobilitis

Dan Kyte

A BAD CASE OF "automobilitis" was passed on to me from my father. He was addicted to anything with four wheels and spent much of his free time browsing used car lots looking for bargains. When I turned fifteen, I asked him when I could have a car of my own. Pop replied that when I had saved $100, he would find me something to drive. I took to the challenge and after working for months on neighboring farms, I finally had my car money. I waited impatiently for Pop to show up with my new ride. Then one afternoon it happened—he came home with a 1952 Ford sedan. It was a six-cylinder automatic and proved to be slow as molasses. Perhaps a safe bet for a teenager intent on speed, but a lost cause for me. This particular product of American engineering wouldn't go 50 mph downhill out of gear. Still, it was a ride of sorts and a start to my car career.

That old Ford was the first of many cars and deals shared with my father. Soon came a WWII 1946 Army Jeep which entertained my high school friends on mountain climbing adventures and overnight campouts. After my first year in high school, I got a job at a local service station working nights and weekends. With the extra money I earned, I sent Pop on a quest for my dream car. He came back one Saturday afternoon with a 1956 Chevy two-door hardtop. It had what was known then as a power pack with a 283 V-8 and a four-barrel carburetor. It was a sight to behold, but unfortunately it was also eaten away by rust, camouflaged by the previous owner with a new coat of paint and skillfully applied Bondo. It was quickly discarded as the search continued for a better choice.

Following the Chevy, I came into possession of a 1965 Mustang fastback with a beautiful white exterior and a red—dare I say red-hot—interior. It proved to be what was referred to in those days as a "chick magnet." One night I was cruising the local mall parking lot looking for a young lady I was keen on, when suddenly out of nowhere, a light pole jumped in front of my Mustang causing major damage. So much for the Mustang. Following this mishap, I enjoyed a succession of cars, including a Triumph Spitfire and a 65 Ford Falcon with a 289 V-8. All of these vehicles were, in part, due to my and my father's shared love affair with the automotive world. I will always be grateful that he passed his attachment on to me, including the life-long disease of automobilitis. Of course, like many other women married to men infected with automobilitis, my wife has expressed her dissatisfaction with my multiple trades over the years. Although at times, my pursuit of the perfect car has adversely affected the family budget, to her credit, she has tolerated my sickness. That said, my most recent purchase of a 2008 Saturn Sky did test the limits of her patience. Still, I press on. What else lies over the next horizon to pique my interest? Electric vehicles? Hmmm.

14 My First Car

Jerry Leger

MY FIRST CAR STARTED out as our family car, a 1955 Studebaker Commander, purchased in Forsyth, Georgia. We did not have a lot of money so Dad bought the bare bones version, which had no air-conditioning or even a radio. At the last minute, he did decided to include a heater, which was located under the passenger's seat. In those days, the bar was low for what passed as a heater. Still, as weak as it was, that heater would prove useful when my family moved to Jamestown, North Dakota in 1957. Winters in North Dakota were frigid with temperatures routinely falling below zero! To combat the bone-numbing cold, Dad installed what he called an electric head-bolt heater that heated the radiator fluid. We kept it continually plugged-in during North Dakota winters.

The Commander was two-toned, white on top and black on the bottom. It had a 259 V-8 engine with a two-barrel carburetor. It was an automatic with only "D" and "L" available to drive it forward. The "R" gear was positioned to the right of the steering column lever. I have never seen that configuration since. A unique feature of the shifter mechanism was a green "jewel" that glowed under the drive letter you selected. which burned out after a year. The Studebaker had no power steering or power brakes. In North Dakota, we kept snow tires on it year-round, which would prove useful when the car was finally passed to me in 1961. Those tires allowed me to easily squeal the rubber due to their design. Burning rubber in a Studebaker may not sound like much of a benefit, but to a teenage boy, it at least gave the impression he was driving a car that was more serious that it appeared to be.

I would drive the car to the Teen Canteen and hang out with friends, listening to my favorite song on the jukebox—Roy Orbison singing "Love Hurts." Later, when the woman who supervised the teen center finally switched the record, she gave it to me, and to this day I still have it in my box of 45's. After Teen Canteen closed, my friends and I would go cruising around town. The Commander's V-8 engine had a little bit of torque so I was able to impress my riders by gunning it, producing loud squealing sounds from the one tire that was closest to the corner. As I have already indicated, those snow tires were easy to spin, especially going around corners!

When I was given the Commander in 1961, I had already been driving a little. But once I got the car, I became known at Jamestown High School as "a guy with a car." In Jamestown, there were two car clubs—the "Road Runners" and the "Road Knights." Of course, just because you had a car didn't mean you were going to be invited to join either one. Even with a "Commander" logo, my ride was clearly inferior and, besides, I was one of the nerdy guys who lacked the coolness factor. The coolest club in town was the Road Runners. They had all the fancy modified, chopped, channeled, chrome-engined cars you could imagine. They wore athletic-style letter jackets, except, rather than having a school name, they had "Road Runners" with a picture resembling the Warner Brothers cartoon Road Runner emblazoned across the back. Road Runners were the coolest guys in the community. Although most of them had graduated from high school, none went on to college. Apparently, they were too busy dating and impregnating the hottest high-school girls. They were lucky that statutory rape was not an issue back then.

When cruising around town, you could always tell if a Road Runner was ahead of you when you came to the railroad tracks. Jamestown was a big railroad town during this era and was served by the Northern Pacific Railroad. It was standard protocol for Road Runners to inch their vehicles over the tracks, thereby minimizing any chances for jarring vibrations. If you were behind them, you just had to pull up a seat and wait for the crossing parade event to conclude. In fact, when my friends and I came to railroad tracks, we would say that we were "road runnering" the car by inching over the rails.

Road Runners were always talking and pontificating about taking their rides to "the coast." Not the east coast, but to California. It was thousands of miles to "the coast," but they wanted to go there so they could cruise through Hollywood. To my knowledge, none of them ever made it to what they perceived to be the west-coast-cruising-promised-land. Still, I guess when one's best days end after high school, new dreams, no matter how unrealistic, are conjured up.

The Road Knights were a second-class car club with first-class pretentions. Their membership was older and their cars lacked the flair of the Road Runners' rides.

One of my friends felt left out of the car club scene and decided that he wanted to form his own club. I forget what name he came up with, but he invited all of us leftover "guys with a car" to a meeting where we spent a lot of time talking about logos and such. I remember in particular when the issue of inviting others to join came up, that a fellow named Glen was mentioned as a possible member. Glen's dad was a local independent mechanic who worked out of his garage located next to his house. Although his father was known as a master mechanic, his property was strewn with all sorts of motors, car shells, transmissions, oil and more oil. Glen was stigmatized because of this, but in the end, it didn't really matter because our wanna-be club folded after the initial meeting.

The aforementioned Glen was a very independent guy who didn't really hang around with anyone. He drove a two door Studebaker coupe and although it was not a Silver or Golden Hawk, it did have the big Studebaker engine with a stick shift so tall that the handle nearly touched the roof. Both sides of his car were lettered with the name, "The Slouch," and there was a painting of a Jiminy Cricket type of character in a top hat, tails, and a long cane. There were also dice hanging from his rear-view mirror. Even though

"The Slouch" was a bit rusted and spent a good deal of time in Glen's dad's garage, it was still a sight to behold.

By this time, my Commander was feeling the wear and tear of teenage cruising. You can only go around so many corners gunning the engine before such a practice catches up with you. The engine finally froze up. I talked my Dad into letting me approach Glen about replacing my engine with the big 289 that was in the now retired "Slouch." Surprisingly, Dad agreed, so I went over to Glen's house to make an offer. He said that before he made a deal, we should go for a ride in "The Slouch" to check out the engine. Glen drove because I didn't know how to drive a stick shift at the time and besides, how on earth does one shift gears when the stick is so tall? So we climbed aboard "The Slouch" and took off. There was a hole in the floorboard right between my legs on the passenger's side and Glen announced that there was no muffler, that exhaust just came out of the manifold into a short pipe that culminated right at that hole. So there we were, driving around with me being carbon monoxized and praying that I would get out of Glen's car alive. Because Glen wanted to demonstrate his car's prowess, we drove around a long time and it's a miracle that I survived. We made the deal anyway and Glen installed the 289 into the Commander. I drove my newly powered Commander for six months until alas, the engine blew up and my Dad decided the Commander was heading to the junkyard.

My first car, a Studebaker Commander: may you rest in peace.

15 A Jeep Named Willys

William Miller

HIGH SCHOOL IS AN in-between time of life, a time when you look like an adult and want the freedom and respect adults have, but still have the remnants, desires, and insecurities of the childhood you are leaving behind. In short, you want the benefits of adulthood without the responsibilities. Sports, parties, girls, and hanging out with friends along with just enough study time to get by is the order of the day. When you turn sixteen and get your driver's license, dreams of acquiring your own "magic carpet ride" quickly move to the front of your ever active imagination. How about a convertible or maybe a two door coup with a V-8 and four-on-the-floor? And don't forget about a tricked-out stereo with the latest 8-track player belting top ten tunes while you cruise down the main drag.

I knew my dad was looking around for a car to give me. With a twinkle in his eye, he would drop a hint here and there at the breakfast or dinner table. On every occasion, I would find myself getting excited, envisioning a new and improved version of what I had been dreaming about the day before.

Finally, the big day came. My father walked into my bedroom, dangling a set of keys and grinning from ear to ear. He led me to the driveway where my chariot awaited. Like a game show host awarding the grand prize, he handed me the keys to a 1948, army surplus Willys Jeep. Extolling its virtues, he pointed out that it had a three-on-the-floor stick shift. Not only that, it also had both high- and low-range four-wheel drive. A new canvas top lay behind the front bucket seats that I would need to figure out how to install. Dad assured me that once it was installed, it could easily be removed so I could enjoy the Jeep as a convertible. Of course, there was one small detail he left out of his lavish vehicle overview—that there was a governor on the engine that didn't allow it to go over 45 mph. Dad ended with a flourish and waited for my response. Of course, I did what any good son would do, I said, "Wow! Thanks, Dad." After all, even an Army surplus Jeep was better than a three-speed bicycle.

Rolling into Hardee's the next Friday night in my new ride was like having a "What the . . . ?" painted bright red on the side of the Jeep. There was John in his 442 Oldsmobile, Keith in his Barracuda, Ellen in the new Cutlass Supreme her Grand-dad had bought her, and Jerry, who was a hippie before being a hippie was cool, leaning on his VW bus. Soon after I got there, Chris pulled up in his Firebird with Jimmy's Camaro right behind him. Polished to a high shine, the car chatter was abundant. They spoke of glittering chrome and mag wheels, a language Willys wasn't familiar with. What they didn't realize at the time, nor did I, was that old Willys had some hidden attributes that their "pretty boy" rides didn't possess.

Camaro Jimmy's parents had a weekend house on Boone Lake. When his parents went out of town, it became the designation of choice for summertime date-night parking. The challenge for the Hardee's crowd was to see how fast we could make the drive. Believe it or not, VW Jerry held the record in just under ten minutes. Maybe, he knew some shortcuts, maybe he didn't. Whatever the case, they could have given me a ten-minute head-start and still beat me. Once we got there, it was a different story. The Jeep's true colors begin to shine when it rained and the cute cars got stuck in the mud. Willys and its low-range four-wheel-drive rescued more than one passionate couple who were running late toward their parents' curfew.

In 1968, January roared in with the first real snowstorm of the year. One Thursday night with eight inches of snow and ice on the ground, good news—no school the next day. Friday morning, everyone was home with no way to get out. Those fancy rides were no match for snow and ice, but old Willys was. I took Dad to work and Coach Little called around to inform all of us that basketball practice would start at 12 noon sharp in the high-school gym. It took Willys and me three trips, but by noon, I had rounded up all 12 players and deposited them in said gym. My Jeep and I were slowly becoming weekend heroes. No matter how much snow and ice, Willys' four-wheel-drive plowed through it without a hitch.

By Saturday night, word had gotten around. I was the only one who had a vehicle that could go in the snow. Dad had bought me that ride because he thought I could not get in much trouble with a vehicle that could not go over 45 miles per hour. He may have been right in theory, but not so much in practice. At 8:30 p.m. on a cold, snowy Saturday night, Willys and I were running up North Roan Street with four friends inside and two others holding on for dear life to a 30-foot to-rope tied to an inner tube. We dragged John and Jerry up the four-lane road and down the parkway in front of the school. I couldn't tell if the shouts I heard from them were screams of joy or terror, and if caught, I might well have lost my ride. Still, for one cold night in January, I was the leader of the pack. Snow covered and frost bitten, my friends hailed the chief, and my Jeep and I made it home just in time to beat my dad's curfew.

16 The Heap

Matt Lawson

"WHO IN THEIR RIGHT mind wants to drive a car?" The question brought our leisurely chatter to a stop.

At the moment, we were all a little drunk and no one was even a tiny bit eager to risk the slick roads or possible DUI checkpoints. Before we could mock the question or object, Justin cut us off, "No, I'm serious. Who wants to drive a damn car anymore?"

The question hung in the air over Justin's leather-encased smart phone that lit up as he navigated the screen with his thumb. "I'm never driving again," Justin said. "Why would I want to?"

"I'll always have a car," Eli replied. "And I'll drive the damn thing, because that's what I do."

"Yeah, and hundreds of years ago people thought they'd always have a horse. Look at what happened to the manual transmission." Justin dismissively retorted. "Technology changes faster than people."

With a final pound on his screen, Justin's phone flashed a sapphire hue and the phone spoke up in an Australian accent, "I'm on my way."

"Just wait. I'll never drive again, and soon, I bet you won't either," he continued as he slid his phone into his back pocket and finished his gin and soda.

"What about when quarantine is over and you have to go back to the office? Are you going to Uber both ways five days a week?" It was the obvious question and I was glad Eli asked it.

"What office?" Justin answers. "My company shut that dump down in June for Covid reasons, and I don't blame them! Think about the money they're saving! No more snacks, coffee, rent, bathroom maintenance. Our profits have never been higher, employee satisfaction is off the charts."

"My company just delayed reopening again," I chimed in. "It will be next year or later."

"You're damn right!" Justin pounded the table for effect. "Work from home is going to be a mandatory benefit if any of these companies want to hire anyone. Period."

Eli waved his hands, "All right, so IF your office reopens OR you change jobs and the new job REQUIRES you to go in the office, you're going to quit driving no matter what? Do we have a name a for a car-bum lifestyle?"

"Hobo-hicular?" I suggested.

"I like that," Eli said with a nod.

"You're one to talk. When is the last time you drove your car?" Justin asked me. "Last time you mentioned it, it didn't even run. Back to your question for me—even IF I get that cruel and unfortunate job that mandates office presence, I will get one of those self-driving cars, so my original point stands. No one wants to drive a car, and soon, no one will."

"Bullshit," Eli said. "Even self-driving cars need some manual control. Just look at all those Tesla accidents."

"Not for long. Trust me," Justin continued, looking at his phone. "Well, it was a fun night, boys," he said, standing up, "but I've got to go. My driver awaits."

Eli and I gave Justin a wave with promises to be safe and talk soon as he exited the bar and got into the car.

"That's a pretty slick looking car." I remarked as it drove away.

"Yeah, it's a good-looking car," Eli admitted. "I mean if you like that style. I prefer things to be more rustic."

For Eli, "rustic" was an understatement. He was that friend who always drove the biggest, boxiest vehicle you've ever ridden in. His ride was only slightly more aerodynamic than a motor home.

When I first met Eli, he was driving a Jeep with an actual set of metal testicles hanging off the trailer hitch, but now he drives a military-grade Hummer with two spare tires and a tailpipe that shoots green flames. He probably paid more for those flames than I've ever spent on a car in my life.

I got my first car when I was 16. My parents picked it up at the dealership on my birthday and drove it home. To me, it was a tan vehicle with four wheels and a tape player, but to them, it was a reliable machine and a wonder to behold. They quickly informed me that they got the champagne version which came with cup holders in the back, followed by a quick warning to tell my friends not to be spilling anything in the back seat.

What do most 16-year-olds do when they get a new car? Jump in, honk the horn, blast some of the day's hottest music and take off for freedom? I wasn't most 16-year-olds. It took me awhile.

After a few hours sitting in the driveway, I decided to drive my new ride to my favorite bookstore. Unfortunately, a few days later I drove it into a parked car. The thing of it is, I didn't understand the magic of cars until a year later, when my friend Joey bought The Heap.

To this day, I can still smell the inside of The Heap and the sensation always perks me up. Nothing else in this world can evoke the combination of oil, cigarettes, and petrified energy drinks into such a thrilling sensation. Even though it pulls the hair on my nostrils, the memory makes me smile, and I can feel my youth wash over me once more.

In a perfect world, The Heap would never have been driven off of the car lot. It should have been towed to Joey's front yard and dropped dead at his feet to become the biggest paperweight the world has ever seen. But after months of receiving the kind of love and attention that can only come from spit, sweat, and the tender massage of his dad's power tools, it was finally able to rev its motor and live again, and live it certainly did.

Everyone in school, maybe even a few counties over, knew about The Heap. If social media had existed then, The Heap and all of its D-grade glory would have gone viral and carried more fans than most celebrities. Other people at school tried to brand their cars with store-bought attitude and trendy nicknames, but they all failed and came up short. The Heap was the champion, the original—the one and only.

After another beer and some wings, Eli offered to give me a ride home in his Hummer. Even though I hated getting in Eli's motorized frat house, given that it was raining, I decided to take him up on his offer.

I have often wondered to myself why they even build such single-story vehicles without a stepladder? Is watching people struggle to get in part of the fun? I often observed how others get in, hoping to pick up some tips, but they all look as foolish as I do. At best, they are limber enough to hop one foot in and pull the other one up. My approach is to swing my ass up and in, while my arms flail around frantically trying to grab something sturdy enough to pull the rest of myself up.

On the ride home, I found myself still thinking about The Heap and that, it came with a radio but speakers which were beyond repair. I guess Joey could have scrimped and saved to get a new sound system, but what he did instead was grab a portable CD player and some extra computer speakers from his room and mount his makeshift system to the dash. It was so innovative and brilliant that I immediately wanted to do the same thing. I soon realized that I could never get it wired as well as Joey's creation. Everything about The Heap was just so damned original that it was almost beyond description.

That's the great thing about being young. The foolish can be brave. The cheap can be daring. The ingenious can be inspired. The different can be memorable. I couldn't imagine being in my 30s someday and getting a ride from somebody with speakers hot glued onto their dashboard.

Like I said, there was only one Heap in the world.

As my condo came into view, I could see the lights were off inside, so my girlfriend would probably be asleep, guarded by her little dog who always growled when someone tried to make him move, especially when that someone was me.

"Thanks for the ride, man!" I said to Eli, popping the door open, checking the ground for a safe landing before hopping out.

"Yup!" Eli said. "See you next week."

As he pulled off, I couldn't help but think how his ride looked like a mobile DJ booth, complete with a thunderous bass and enough neon lights to have an electricity bill. If it were not for the sleep altering sound and lightshow, it would be a thrilling sight.

Settling in for the night, my thoughts returned to The Heap. It was a wreck of a car, sure, but it was a hobo's delight, and Joey really thought every feasible accommodation through. I mean, he always had whatever you needed in that car:

- portable speakers, check
- snacks in the dash, check
- rolling papers, check
- sunglasses, check
- an odd and generous amount of loose change, check
- jumper cables and first aid, check
- blanket and pillows, check
- weapons…umm…check? Nothing comes to mind, I'm sure he could pull something together for whatever need might arise.

One of the best nights of our young lives was when Joey took The Heap down to Race Nights. I remember him sneaking it into the show line and popping the engine cover shoulder to shoulder with all of the other rubber burners like you see in movies and on TV. The best part was observing all of the confused spectators trying to figure out The Heap's engine, like it was some kind of complex mechanical puzzle they couldn't quite decipher. I even overheard one of the older guys whisper to his girlfriend, "I think this car is a piece of shit, but I'm honestly not sure."

Now that I think back, I love that the guy was capable of giving Joey that much credit. It's like he knew that technology would get ahead of him and maybe The Heap's questionable mechanics and Joey's Tenacious D shirt were a smoke screen for the birth of the first aerospace inspired roadster.

No one knew how seriously to take The Heap that night until Joey paid the $25 to enter the race and pulled up to the starting line. He was the talk of the track. Cameras lit up. Rumors swirled that The Heap was a dark horse and going to hit Mach 1—probably because we brought a handmade sign that said as much.

When the handkerchief dropped, Joey slammed on the gas like his foot was trying to stop a leak in the *Titanic*. The Heap screeched to life and matched our wildest expectations, topping out at a groaning 93 mph. The crowd, now in on the joke, went crazy. The Heap bellied up for three races that night and miraculously won one of them. I still wonder if the guy that lost was playing nice or actually got beat after a dreadful start. No one could tell from his reaction and he didn't stick around for questions.

At school the next day, everyone wanted to take a turn in The Heap with Joey. The hottest drug dealers, the jazziest band members, and the cutest girls—they all wanted to break bad and take a spin in the car their parents warned them about. There were tons of rich kids and slick cars, but there was only one Heap, and it was glorious for all the wrong reasons.

I lost touch with Joey. I do know that The Heap didn't survive college and I guess Joey's budding reputation didn't do much better. I don't think either of them met a grisly demise, but in The Heap's final days, it probably became more expensive to fix than it was worth.

There's a part of me that wishes The Heap was in the city's museum or some other place like that. I can't imagine that there will ever be anything else on four wheels like it. And I still can't imagine ever getting into another car with computer speakers hot glued to dashboard. The Heap was an original.

17 A Wild Maverick

Jeffrey Walker

LIKE MANY TEENAGED BOYS, I wanted a hot rod. I dragged my dad around to a lot of places where we scrutinized all kinds of cars, including a six-cylinder Camaro, a four-speed (but four-cylinder) Mustang, and a pretty normal Nova with a small V-8. He shot them all down. He knew what I wanted, especially since I had two older brothers, but he was not about to let me have the hot rod of my dreams.

Then we found a little Ford Maverick sitting on a car lot a friend of his owned. The Maverick was a very baseline compact car, little more than a dressed-up Pinto. Maybe that's why he agreed to this one. Whatever his reason, I was finally in business. Although it had a V-8 engine and a shifter on the floor, what he didn't know (and neither did I) was that this was the Grabber edition of the Maverick. It looked fairly normal except it was red with white striping. So, it looked a little racy. What I learned later was that this edition of the Maverick had the same 302 V-8 and the same C4 transmission as the top-of-the-line Mustang. In other words, "the race was on."

To make money for the car, gas, and going out, I took a job as a janitor at the local vocational-technical school. I soon got to know the people who worked there, especially the people in the auto mechanics program. So, when I got my Maverick, I knew I had people to help me fix it up. I imagined that since it was painted red, it would go faster. All I needed were some modifications. It was then that I got the second big break in my hot-rod life. Apparently, God wanted me to have a hot rod, because not long after that, my high-school counselor came around to classes offering a program where you could attend regular classes a half day and spend a half day at the Vo-Tech school. I already had all of the credits I needed to graduate, so much to my mother's dismay, I jumped at the offer.

Now I had a car, and I had a degree to teach me how to make it—stealing a line from *Smoky and the Bandit*, speedy, "speedier than that." After a few paychecks, I made the first modification. I went to the tire shop my dad used where they were selling tires to people who were into dirt track racing. The big thing with the other kids who were building hot rods was a 60 series tire. It was much wider than normal tires. But I wasn't going to settle for a 60 series tire. No, no! I wanted a pair of 50 series, race tires. At first, the tire shop wouldn't sell them to me because they wouldn't fit my car. I thought about getting air shocks, which is how most kids jacked their cars up. But they were expensive, and most people I talked to complained about how they were a problem. Instead, I started digging around and found one of the guys who said I should get "shackles" for my car. This was a modification that was fairly common in the 1950s. Basically, you unbolted the rear part of the rear shocks, then bolted two metal plates with holes in them between the shock and the frame of the car. This technique jacked the car up for $15 instead of paying $160 for regular air shocks. After bolting them on, I went back to the tire shop. With the cash I had saved, I could get the bigger chrome wheels I wanted. That was in 1979, and to this day, I remember what the shop owner said when he walked out and looked at the back of my little Maverick with those huge dirt track tires under it. "It looks like a bull with sore balls." It may have looked that way to him, but I was in heaven.

Now, my baby was jacked up and had huge tires and four chrome wheels. It was starting to look like a real racer. Next job was the exhaust system. All of the hot rods in town had dual exhausts. It made the cars (and trucks) louder--you know, like a race car. So, I started saving my paychecks for dual exhausts. Once again, the stars lined up for my hot rod. My little town had a speed shop that sold chrome parts, wheels, and all things speedy. One day, when I was in there talking with the owner, I fell in love with a set of chrome side pipes (in the 1950s they were called lake pipes). I packed those up and headed to the Vo-Tech where one of my buddies put the pipes on for free.

The outside was now complete. If you looked at my Maverick from the side, it was chrome front wheels, chrome side pipes that ran from the front wheels to the back wheels, and chrome back wheels. Add in the red paint, and it spelled s-p-e-e-d. If you looked at it from the back, all you could see was the huge rear wheels. It may not have been the fastest car in town, but it sure looked the part. And with the trick of blowing out the ballasts in the mufflers that were inside the side pipes, it also sounded the part. Oh, what fun I had cruising main street on the weekends.

Finally, it was time to start working on true speed. The first thing that had to go was the carburetor. It came with a two-barrel carburetor. That would not do. My next move was to go to the junk yard, where I spent an enormous amount of my time and money over the next few years. The owner allowed me to look around at wrecked cars and pull parts if I found what I needed. I came across an old Mustang that had a Holley brand "double pumper" four-barrel carburetor. I couldn't believe my good luck. Just that piece alone made my Maverick go a lot faster, and, heck, gas was cheap then, so I didn't care about gas mileage.

When we weren't working on other people's cars as part of my auto mechanics program, we were either working on a complete rebuild of a 1928 Model A or my car. We spent about a week changing the "jets" in the carburetor. The jets were what put more or less gas into the engine. We didn't have a machine to test horsepower changes, so we would change the jets and I would run my Maverick down a nearby piece of straight highway and time it. We probably put in 25 or more different jet combinations before we got the best time. Now my little Maverick was ready to be a drag racer. It still wasn't as fast as some of the other cars, but fortunately, the local drag strip had "bracket racing" where you got a head start if you were the slower car. The drag strip was lots of fun--until my dad found out. I had also started putting race kits in the transmission, changed out the rear end and was always looking for something to change in the engine. It was more than a hobby—it was my life. There was even a picture in my high-school yearbook where I was lying on the hood and leaning back on the windshield. The caption read "Walker loves his car."

18 Growing Up Buick

Pete Kilbourne

WHEN I WAS BORN, my dad was managing an Esso service station which later became Exxon. Three years later, he left Esso and built and operated a Buick dealership for General Motors. When I was eight years old, I was sent to the "garage" after school to be with my dad. I guess you could call it an early version of what is now referred to as day care. The long and short of it is I have been around cars all my life.

My first job at the Buick day care center was wiping grease and oil from the floor. After that, I was promoted to a push broom. Since I didn't mess up those tasks too badly, I moved up to cleaning the showroom windows. By the time I was ten, I was transferred to the parts department. Parts weren't really my thing. I just couldn't get excited about dealing with seven-digit numbers all day long, much less waiting, then waiting some more, for a customer or mechanic to need a part. *Boring* is one word that comes to mind.

Like many sons, I was always trying to please my dad and gain his approval and respect. While pondering my various jobs at the dealership, I figured out one of life's great lessons: If you don't want to keep doing an assigned task, don't do a good job. If you do, it will be your job from then on. I used this newly-discovered rule of work to get out of the parts department. I wouldn't really mess up, but occasionally, I would just take too long to find a part or look up a cross-over part number. Eventually, that got on my dad's nerves just enough to get me transferred to another assignment.

Next stop, the car wash bay. By then, I was tall enough to reach all areas of the cars so I could be fairly efficient at washing a car within a reasonable length of time. Also, when I got bored, I could move over to the used car lot and wash some of those cars as well. I liked this much better. Happy days were here again.

One day, when I had turned 13, my dad took me to the wheel balancing machine and showed me, in great detail, how to balance a tire. In those days, the wheel and tire were removed from the car and mounted on the balancing machine. Dad was a good teacher, and I didn't know it until later that he was not only teaching me how to balance a tire but was also testing me.

He started out showing me how to adjust the bridle to the proper spacing of the lug holes so the tire could be firmly mounted to the spindle of the balancing machine. After removing all of the existing wheel weights, he checked to make sure that the wheel was flat. He did this by holding a piece of chalk next to the rim while spinning the tire by hand. At the same time, he explained that you can't balance a tire that isn't flat. He meticulously moved through the rest of the process, adding and re-positioning the wheel weights.

To check the tire's balance, a spinning drive wheel was pulled up to the bottom of the tire and the tire was spun at a speed equivalent to 50 mph. If it wasn't balanced, the tire would wobble and a static arc would show in the position circle. By correctly reading the position of the static arc, one could figure out where to place a wheel weight. It was all fascinating. Hey, I was getting a chance to do some real mechanic work, not just clean things.

Finally, after he had balanced the tire, he turned to me and asked, "Have you got this?" When I said, "yes," he pointed to a second tire lying in the floor, and walking toward his office, he told me to balance it. His office was adjacent to the wheel balancing machine and was elevated about two steps above the shop floor, giving him a clear view of my activities.

During the next couple of hours I placed and removed nearly every weight in the weight box. I was sure that I had understood my dad's explanation of how to read the static arc. Although I was also confident in my understanding of whether to place the weight on the inside of the wheel or the outside, I just couldn't come up with the right combination that would balance the tire.

Believing I had suffered enough, my dad finally appeared with the fatherly inquiry; "How are you doing, son?" I explained that I was having a lot of trouble as he started removing all of the weights I had added to the wheel. He then reached for the chalk and I knew that I had been had. The wheel was a half inch out of flat and could, in fact, never be balanced. Dad knew that. He was testing me to see how well I had listened to him. Besides, that wheel balancer had kept me occupied for most of the afternoon next to Dad's office where he could keep an eye on me. It turned out to be one of several good lessons I learned at his dealership.

Spending those afternoons in the garage exposed me to cars of all types. Looking back, I can't recall if I was born with a mechanical inclination or if it was ingrained in me because of my time working in the garage. Perhaps it was a little of both. Whatever the reason, to this day, I am interested in learning what makes a machine or gadget work. Even though I was always around cars, I didn't get "car fever" until later in my life. To me, cars were just things you washed, swept out, or worked on.

When I was 11, my dad came home one day for lunch. After we ate, he told me to come outside with him. Standing there in the driveway was a 1946 Willys Jeep like the army used. We got in and Dad drove to the front steps of the church across the street. After driving up the steps in the Jeep, he explained the difference between a four-wheel drive Jeep and a regular automobile. After conquering that small feat, we went back to our yard, where Dad proceeded to drive around the house, down through the trees, and up the hill in front of the house. Halfway up the hill, he stopped and turned off the key, set the emergency brake, and took his feet off the pedals. Then he said, "Now, watch this," and starting the engine, he drove to the top of the hill without rolling backwards or spinning the tires.

After making a round or two, he stopped the Jeep, looked at me and said, "Now, you do it". So, I did. I made a circuit or two, including the stopping-on-the-hill exercise in a way that must have pleased him. He motioned for me to stop and got out of the Jeep with the instructions that I was to stay in the yard, and if I got into trouble, to turn off the ignition. Whereupon, he left and went back to work. I spent the rest of the afternoon circling our house and driving among the many maple trees that populated the yard. Needless to say, I was hooked. From that moment on, I had car fever.

We lived in coal country and things went along pretty well until 1956 when the mine owners mechanized the mines and laid off hundreds of miners. At that point, life went south. Because most of the working population in our town were miners, selling Buicks got a lot more difficult.

During the next three years, Buick made the three worst automobiles ever produced by General Motors. Quality control was non-existent and selling Buicks was nearly impossible. The following year, General Motors changed all of the management team in its Buick Motor Division, turned things around, and started making good automobiles again. I can still remember the old Buick motto: "When better automobiles are built, Buick will build them." Well, they finally righted the ship, but it was too late for my dad's dealership.

One of the more dramatic changes the new Buick management made had to do with engine durability. They would pull 100 engines at random from their assembly line and disassemble them for inspection. If they found a problem, say a tight pin, they noted it and reassembled the engine. Each engine was then tested in a wind tunnel under a load equivalent to driving a car down a level road at 60 mph until it failed. The longest time recorded was less than a minute! Needless to say, Buick fixed this and other problems and, as a result, survived. Buick survived, but it was too much for Dad. His business was sold at auction.

In those days, "heart healthy" eating and living weren't on the radar for most folks. Three years later, my dad died of a heart attack. I was a freshman in college and my infatuation with cars had to be put on hold for a while, since my means of transportation was limited to hitchhiking back and forth to school.

When my mother finally probated Dad's will, she learned that she had inherited some of his used cars. She wanted to give me one to drive back and forth to college so I picked out a 1956, two-door Biscayne Chevrolet with an automatic transmission.

Not knowing where it came from or what shape it was in, I thought it was a good deal. Shortly after receiving it, I found that it needed a new engine. One of Dad's former mechanics tried to help me out, selling me an engine he had on hand and installing it in the Chevy.

The summer after Dad died, I worked hard at fixing up the car. I put new metal in the floorboards, installed new carpet, and installed new gauges to monitor oil pressure and water temperature. After applying a coat of wax, I had to admit that I had become pretty attached to the Chevy. I was ready to ride.

All in all, I made 13 trips to college in that car. Unfortunately, there were seven trips that I didn't make. For all its good looks, the Biscayne had a critical flaw. The new motor didn't match up correctly with the bell housing of the transmission, so whenever I drove it, oil leaked out continuously. On average, I had to stop every 46 miles to refill the oil. Needless to say, the new oil pressure gauge really came in handy. Since I was in college, I had very little money and would often ask service stations for their used oil to top off my car.

Was I foolish to keep my oil sucking Chevy for so long? There were other problems as well—a water pump here and a generator there. All of my friends said I was throwing good money after bad. Why didn't I trade and get a better car? Why was I being so hardheaded? Well, I didn't think I was being stubborn. I simply had no money and could make it work—kinda, sorta.

After all, we were talking about my first car! For many of us, where first cars are concerned, you take what you can get and make the best of it.

19 The Mercury Man

Robert Brassell

I HAVE BEEN FASCINATED by cars since I was a young boy of seven or eight. I can remember sitting on the concrete steps of the stone wall fronting our street and watching all the cars of the late '50s and early '60s drive by. Although our street was not heavily traveled, a steady stream of automobiles rolled by. I prided myself on recognizing each passing car by its front or rear, and stating out loud to myself, or anyone listening, "That's a '55 Chevy!" or a "'56 Cadillac!" There were always a few neighbors' cars parked on each side of the street, which we had to navigate during our football, wiffle ball baseball games, or hide and seek, played in the street during the day, or games like "kick the can" at dusk, until we were called inside our homes for dinner. We were lucky to always have enough neighborhood friends to play with outdoors.

One father. One mother. Twelve kids! That was us. If you're old enough to remember the movie *Cheaper by the Dozen*, then you have an idea of the constant chaos that a large family can bring. Our parents added a whimsical touch by having all our middle names begin with the letter "J," my father included.

Automobiles continued to become part of my life's storyline, synonymous with events, school, parties, trips to hospitals, dates to movie theatres or drive-ins, hanging out at curb-side, dining at Shoney's or the Krystal. Cars were essential for just riding around, listening to music with friends, maybe drinking and singing along uninhibited to the songs we knew, or making up lyrics that we thought rhymed. The memories that follow represent bits and pieces of those cars, and how some were integral to certain significant moments of my life.

My dad had Fords for a while, probably influenced by my brother-in-law, who worked for Ford. I believe the first family car we owned, when I was maybe eight or nine years old, was a 1947 or '48 black Ford Coupe. It had a tan fabric interior and a push-button starter and remained parked in front of our house, much like a solemn sentry, for several years spanning the late 1950s. I can't recall this car ever moving from its assigned parking spot. I do remember sitting in the musty smelling dust-covered seats, pretending to drive or reading the latest DC comic books or a book from the library. I wanted to read everything I could. It was a quiet place for me to escape, to concentrate, or just daydream.

My fondest memory of this car was participating in the "paper drives" we had at my elementary school, an annual contest that introduced me to a new world of competition outside of sports. The student that brought in the largest number of old newspapers was given first prize bragging rights for a full year! Several of my older brothers and sisters were already recent champions, so they put pressure on me to continue this legacy. I remember going from house to house with my Radio Flyer metal wagon, begging every neighbor for their used newspapers and asking them to hold next week's until I could return to collect them. Most happily agreed. The red wagon with tall removable wooden rails allowed me to carry a full load of papers back home. The quiet Ford coupe became the staging area for the papers until the designated day arrived to bring them all to school. I had filled every inch of that car's interior and trunk! I won that year by a sizable margin—my first real victory!

We moved to a new home in a quiet neighborhood right before I turned 12 years old. One of the boys, my next-door neighbor, became my best friend. He also encouraged my wild side. His father frequently bought 1955, '56, and '57 Chevys to repair, detail, and resell for a nice profit. He opened a used car dealership on Gallatin Road, and my friend and I would often take a car from his lot at night for a joy ride. When my friend finally totaled one, that practice came to an end.

Our next family car began a series of Mercury automobiles that my dad owned from the early to late 1960s. The 1952 Mercury Sedan is only a vague memory, sitting like a formidable, chromed consumer tank on the grassy area next to our driveway. It was two-toned black and beige, a design that introduced me to "fender skirts."

When I was around 14, we replaced that car with a bright red and white 1956 Mercury Sedan. It was a real beauty with white and red-trimmed leather interior. The seats also were covered with clear form-fitted plastic to protect them from wear and tear. On a hot day, our clammy skin would stick to them. This striking vehicle had fender skirts and wide whitewall tires. The car was also equipped with a large after-market air conditioner protruding from under the radio and resting just above the center floorboard. I believe this was before we even had our first home window air conditioner. Two of my brothers primarily drove this car, mostly to our high school and their jobs. I remember hearing that someone stole it one day from the school parking lot and totaled it. I never saw the wrecked version because I wanted my memory to be of how bold and beautiful this car originally was.

The mid-60s came with one of my favorite cars because it was the first one that I actually got to drive. It was our 1962 Mercury Monterey, painted yellow (my dad's favorite color) with a black convertible top and black leather interior, and an automatic floor shifter console situated between two bucket seats. It had a mighty 390 horsepower engine with a four-barrel carburetor. It was a very heavy car with lots of chrome. It was slow out of the gate, but once it got rolling, it was very fast. I loved "peeling rubber" and drag-racing with friends. I shared driving privileges for this car with a couple of my siblings, but it became primarily mine when I was around 17. I worked part-time at a grocery store just so I could buy gasoline for this very thirsty machine. Gas was 25 cents a gallon which was a lot for me, since I only earned 50 cents an hour. I bought used retread tires that cost $1.00 each, and it seemed that

I had to replace a "baloney-skin" flat tire every week. The rest of my paycheck went for cigarettes—also a quarter for a pack—or to spend frugally on cheap dates. I loved this car! The '62 survived a few minor scrapes, but it couldn't survive being hit by two cars that ran a red light at an intersection downtown. The other cars were also totaled, but this massive hunk of metal kept me from serious harm.

The final Mercury belonging to my father was a 1966 Monterey. It was also a yellow car, but had a white convertible top and white interior. This was my favorite car to drive when I took a special girl on a date, primarily because it had a wide bench seat so my date could sit close to me while I drove or parked. It also had a giant back seat, which I came to appreciate. Although it was still my father's car, though he seldom drove it, it became my primary auto until I moved away from home. The Monterey was part of many adventures through my teen years, and as I developed relationships and special friendships, some, gratefully, that are still around today.

I loved hanging out with my close friends in those days and nights, which usually ended up with us drinking in the car or at a bar. One night, after several pitchers of beer at a favorite pizza place, I threw up on the front floorboard. I was in no condition to drive, and the car was disgusting. One of my "kind" friends decided to drive the car to a self-service car wash. He thought it was a good idea to spray wash the inside of the car with me in it, since I was too intoxicated to move. There were other times when I was too drunk to drive, and my friends carried me from the car to the door of my downstairs bedroom. My mother always knew when I arrived in this condition, waiting at the front door and giving my friends hell for getting me drunk!

My father worked the second shift at the post office, and I generally had to pick him up after work around 11p.m. I frequently ran late, so I made sure my date always sat between me and my father to soften his displeasure at my being late. He could really become irritated with me, but he loved chatting with my girlfriends, so my strategy worked most of the time.

I will always connect the Mercury years to my father, who loved to ride in his cars with the top down. He was conservatively stylish and usually wore a hat on those drives. Along the way he taught me many things about being a responsible man, a good listener, how to enjoy the printed word, and to treat people with kindness and respect. He was self-educated after the eighth grade, but he could carry on a conversation with just about anyone because he had learned so much by reading. He and I often played a game of words. He would say a word, and I would have to spell it and tell him what it meant. I tested him the same way and seldom stumped him. These sessions encouraged me to read much of our huge *Webster's Unabridged Dictionary* and the set of *Encyclopedia Britannica* we were fortunate to have during my early teen years.

Yes, my father was indeed the Mercury Man! He was a little bit of each car, conservative but also flamboyant. I laughed at his dry wit, cried with him during our hard times, sang with him when he played his guitar, and treasured the moments when the two of us were alone late at night after his work and my dates and wild times. He and I would talk about life until the early hours of the morning.

20 My Camaro Romance

Bob Roberson

LIKE MOST YOUNG MEN, I fell in love with automobiles early in life. Batman's Batmobile, the Green Hornet's souped-up Chrysler, and cars driven by other heroes caught my attention and piqued my imagination. I even dreamed of one day using my car for supernatural events. Of course, that never happened but I have never stopped dreaming!

The first car I got to consider at least "part" mine, was a 1957 Ford Fairlane. I didn't get to drive it until 1962, but it was still classy looking to me. The sleek body style with the V-shaped chrome line down the side and the black and gold paint made it stand out. Powered by a 292 CID engine, it could hold its own with most stock "family cars." The first car I actually owned was a 1958 Chrysler Windsor, a boat of a vehicle with huge sweeping fins in the back. I bought it in 1966 to drive from Arizona to Texas for college. The trunk space would hold everything I owned and more, and with the 353 CID engine, the Chrysler could eat up the Texas highways. It had a roomy front bench seat and pushbutton controls on the left side of the dash. This beast of a car would easily carry nine people crammed into the front and back seats. The scenery zoomed by each time I drove through the deserts of west Texas, traveling between my parents' home and college.

After the Fairlane and Chrysler, I finally got the car of my dreams. When I graduated from Abilene Christian College in 1968, my dad gave me a choice of several cars which he was willing to buy as a graduation present. I settled on a 1968 Camaro which cost him $2,800. Fire-engine red with a white vinyl top, the car was a joy to behold. I picked it up about three weeks after my graduation in May of 1968. The Camaro only had 14 miles on it and I immediately drove it from Sierra Vista to Flagstaff, Arizona. Being still relatively young and somewhat immature and reckless, only God could have made me look ahead in time to slam on my brakes and stop sliding about three inches from the back of a car in a long line of cars stopped at a red light. I hadn't been paying attention, and the thought that I could have wrecked it my first time out of town should have taught me an important life lesson. Unfortunately, some people learn more slowly than others.

It grieved me to have to leave my car with my younger brother when I enlisted in the Air Force. I went Camaro-less until I graduated from basic training. After advanced training, I drove to Dover Air Force Base in Delaware where I spent most of the next two years. I remember meeting up with my brother at Ft. Bragg in North Carolina on one occasion, and driving non-stop to Arizona for Christmas. That was a fun trip with the two of us taking turns driving. From Dover, I went to Vietnam and again left my car in the care of my brother. He did a good job of preserving it for me, and it was ready when I got back stateside a year later. I was stationed at Lackland Air Force Base in Albuquerque upon my return from Vietnam and moved into my new quarters in the middle of a snowstorm. From the jungles of Vietnam to a snowstorm in New Mexico—a mind-bending change in both weather and living arrangements.

Driving my Camaro all over the east coast while at Dover and then all over New Mexico turned some heads. While it was only the stock 327 V-8 engine with a three-speed stick on the floor, it still growled nicely and drew its share of attention. Given my lead foot, there were, of course, a few unfortunate times when it drew the wrong type of attention.

As much as I loved that car, it did let me down on one occasion. Driving down a back road named Charleston Road outside Sierra Vista one day, a Dodge Challenger pulled up alongside, tooted its sissy sounding horn, revved its engine, and took off. Well, far be it from me to ignore such a challenge. I put the pedal to the metal. Even pegging the speedometer, the Dodge still pulled away. I never knew what was in that Challenger, but it left me behind and for a moment, took the wind out of my sails.

While attending law school in Tucson, Arizona, my girlfriend Debbie, now my wife, and I, along with her cousin and another friend, were driving around and decided to take a trip out to what we called Roller Coaster Road. The old road was west of I-10 and headed out into the desert. As the name implies, the road was up and down all the way into the desert west of Tucson. There were no houses or lights anywhere along the way, so I floored it and off we went. Topping each rise, the car would fly a few feet before settling back down on the road. Several miles out, Debbie cried out in alarm, "The pavement ends!" And, sure enough, it did. It ended at a ditch which we hit nose first at about 80 mph. The car bounced and lurched out of the other side of the ditch and we finally rolled to a stop. Fortunately, we were all okay, even though this was long before anyone wore seatbelts. I managed to get the car turned around and eased it back through the ditch until we got back on the paved road, heading back toward the Interstate. We hadn't gone a mile on the Interstate when every light on my dash came on and the car abruptly stopped running. I pulled off to the side, got out and popped the hood. There was a layer of dirt and sand covering the top of the engine and the fanbelt had come off. I pried the belt back into place, got back in and started the car. It ran fine. Even to this day, my wife and I occasionally think back to that encounter and thank God we are still alive. I'm not sure her cousin ever rode with me again, although I could hardly blame her.

I loved that Camaro. My wife tells people, even today, that she knew how much I loved her when I let her drive the car by herself. My love affair with that car never really ended, but I finally gave it up in 1975 when I graduated from law school. After scoring my first job as a lawyer, I bought a new 1975 Pontiac Trans-Am. Although I ended up owning six more Trans-Am's after that and enjoyed driving all of them, nothing will ever replace my 1968 Camaro.

A noteworthy postscript: A client in Yuma, Arizona, couldn't afford my bill on time and asked if I would take his car as security against getting paid. I agreed and he drove up to my house in a stripped 1968 Camaro! The paint had been sanded off and the insides stripped of all the carpet and roof lining, but it ran great! I drove that car for about four months, hoping against hope that my client would one day call to tell me to keep it because he couldn't pay my bill. Sadly, he did pay and I had to let the diamond-in-the-rough Camaro go. But, at least for a few months, I relived driving my first new car which in a way, was also my first love.

21 Thunder Road and Beyond

Susan Braswell

MY FATHER WAS A "finder of things." From a motorless yellow school bus he had pulled in our backyard, which served as a playhouse, to refurbished go-carts his grandsons raced around the yard pretending to be Grand Prix drivers—even a souped up vintage 1960s golf cart that was prone to sling passengers from their seat when making a sharp turn, he loved to tinker with this and that.

The most interesting things he found to my way of thinking, were my first two cars. My father taught me to drive on an old dirt road outside of town. It was a straight shot, several miles long. The local teen and drag racing crowd called it "Thunder Road." I never had a car in high school like some of my classmates, and when I went to college, I caught rides home and back to school with older classmates. If they saw a white cloth tied to the pecan tree in our front yard, they would stop to pick me up.

One day, my father "the finder" found my first car, a black two-door 1957 Chevrolet. He proudly informed me that it had a V-8 engine and a straight drive transmission. More than that, a false compartment had been welded underneath the back floorboard to carry moonshine. It may not have been as pretty or exciting as some of the convertibles parked on campus, but no one else to my knowledge drove a black, two-door, moonshine runner. It stood out among the regular modes of transportation and inspired my friends and me to imagine it eluding Sheriff's deputies or dragracing down Thunder Road.

After my student teaching was completed, I was hired for a teaching position in Atlanta. My father informed me he didn't want me to start my new job in the big city driving an old moonshine runner, so he had found me another car. I was excited when he told me he had gotten a great deal on a red Chevrolet Malibu. That was the good news. The bad news was that it had previously been submerged in a nearby lake. My friends and I still laugh about the strange damp and fishy smell that was ever-present in its interior.

When I got settled in Atlanta, I could finally purchase my very own car, a brand-new gold Pontiac Firebird with a beige vinyl top. It had a V-8 engine and an automatic transmission, and I paid it off in three years. For a hundred dollars a month, I had a choice of one option when I signed the papers, a vinyl top or air conditioning.

Who needs air conditioning in the deep south when you can have a snazzy vinyl top?

22 Nice While It Lasted

Bob Wilson

CARS WERE A BIG deal when I went to high school in Nashville in the 1960s. They shined a bright spotlight on which social clique a fellow belonged to: a greaser in a '57 Chevy, a spoiled stud with a new high-powered Camaro or Mustang, a nerd with a Rambler, or a mostly-left-out kid who had to rely on his parents' car when they could spare it. I was in the latter group and usually had to drive my mom's stodgy '58 Chrysler, an out-of-style Grandma-mobile with giant fins, which was the furthest thing from a Camaro or Mustang one could imagine. My friends and the girls at Shoney's derisively referred to it as the "Blue Fin." During those years, cruising Shoney's was a social ritual in our part of Nashville, the place to see and be seen. We would drive repeatedly around the oval of outdoor carhop booths and maybe eventually pull into one to order a Big Boy and a shake. After a few humiliating point-and-laugh experiences from other patrons, I gave up. I would park the Fin in an out-of-the-way place and look for a friend who had an empty seat in a more socially acceptable ride.

Mom still had the Blue Fin in 1970 when I went away to college in Florida. When I came home for Christmas, my parents had finally traded up to a '67 Pontiac Catalina. That car is still my favorite of all the cars that they or I owned. The Catalina still didn't look anything like a Mustang, but it was beautifully styled and handled well. It looked like it came right out of a commercial filmed on the Pacific Coastal highway, driven by a gorgeous blonde with the windows rolled down and her hair flowing in the wind. It was comfortable and roomy and had a huge back seat. I was only home for two weeks on break, but I immediately fell in love with the car and was sad that I wouldn't get to drive it again until summer.

The car was still just as beautiful and sexy when I got home six months later. I found a summer job at a produce wholesaler in downtown Nashville, bought a motorcycle to drive to work, and enjoyed using the Pontiac for dates on weekends. It felt great to pick up a date in a beautiful car. I have to admit that was a pretty terrific summer. In early August, a couple of weeks before I was due to return to college, my twin same-age cousins and I headed out in the Pontiac for a Saturday trip to a state park in Manchester which was a couple of hours down I-24. We ate barbecue, swam in the river below a waterfall, and just generally enjoyed the day before heading back in midafternoon.

We were about halfway home when the temperature light came on. There were no gauges on the Pontiac for engine status, just idiot lights. We debated whether to pull over or try to make it to the next exit. If we had stopped where we were, there would be no way to call for service or a tow. Cell phones weren't invented yet and we were far from a pay phone. So, I turned the A/C off, opened the windows, and turned the heater on to try to help the motor out. The next exit with a gas station was maybe five miles ahead. When I pulled up the ramp and stopped at the stop sign, the engine conked out and steam came pouring out from under the hood. After walking over to the gas station and calling Dad, he called a tow truck to take it to our local garage, then came to get us.

The mechanic called on Monday to give Dad the bad news. The overheating had been caused by a bad thermostat which was pretty common in those days. But my continued driving had caused the heat to build up to the point where the head was warped. Given that the car would need a full valve job and the head reworked, it would be cheaper to install a rebuilt engine in it. My folks took me back to college a couple of weeks later, pulling my motorcycle on a little trailer. By the time I came home for Christmas, the Catalina was all fixed and just as beautiful as before.

A combination of 18-year-olds being able to vote in states like Florida where I was attending college, lowering the drinking age to 18, and the Vietnam draft resulted in my developing a bar habit. Tennessee had also lowered the drinking age to 18 so I was happy to continue my habit over breaks.

The first weekend home I called Sam, a friend whom I had met at work the previous summer. We agreed to meet at a pizza place he frequented near his parents' home on the opposite side of Nashville. We shared a pitcher of beer, had some pizza, and then had another pitcher of beer. I don't know about Sam's condition, but by the time we parted, I had definitely exceeded my limit. The way home led me through Shelby Park, a popular spot in East Nashville in the daytime. At night, it was mostly used as a shortcut between East Nashville and my neighborhood of Inglewood. The roads through the park were winding and not well lit. Although I was obeying the park's 15-mile-an-hour speed limit, it wasn't enough to compensate for my share of the two pitchers of beer we drank. In short, I passed out.

I woke up when the car shook violently as it came to a stop. At first, I wondered if there had been an earthquake. Then I peered out through the windshield and saw a broken 20-foot wooden light pole leaning over the car's crumpled front end. I glanced around and saw nobody. The driver's side door was jammed, but to my surprise, the electric window rolled down. I crawled out and considered what my next move should be. Another car drove by and stopped. After asking me if I was okay, the driver gave me a ride to the nearest convenience store where I knew there would be a pay phone. I called a cab and rode home to my parents' house, conjuring up a cover story. I would tell them a car had come around the opposing side of the S-turn in the park and its bright lights blinded me and caused me to hit the light pole. Even worse, the imaginary car had not stopped. Dad worked nights and Mom had gone to bed, so nobody was available to question my story. I called the police and reported the wreck, and told them my version of events.

When the officer asked if I could come down to the station and fill out a report, I explained that I had taken a cab home and had no way to get there until my dad got back from work in the morning. The officer agreed that I could just come in the next day so I went to bed.

In the morning, I repeated my story to my parents. Although it was plausible, Dad was still pretty mad. I used his car to go to the police station and fill out the report where I repeated my story once more. They didn't ask if I had been drinking or challenge anything I said. Since no other vehicle was involved and the wreck was in such an isolated location, they didn't even question my leaving the scene. As a result, I left without getting a ticket.

Dad didn't have much to say to me for the rest of my break, but a couple of weeks after I returned to college, he seemed a little friendlier on phone calls. Mom explained that Dad had been thinking about trading the car anyway. He worked at a Ford dealership and had decided that he should drive a Ford product to support the brand. He bought a late model Ford LTD. When the insurance check for the Catalina came in, it was for more than he had planned to ask for the car and as a result, he ended up pretty happy about the whole affair.

The only consequences I really suffered were the loss of my beloved Catalina, and its substitution for a car that I really detested. The LTD was an awful design. Its low-slung body with high sidewalls and a low roof meant the window glass was narrower than on most cars and visibility wasn't good. I was over six feet tall and looking out through the front windshield, I couldn't even see the front of the hood which sloped downward. I also couldn't see much out of the back window if I was backing up. The handling was clunky, and unlike the Catalina's smooth take-off, the throttle response was jerkily. The LTD had a black vinyl roof which was already becoming faded. In retrospect, that car made me a lifelong hater of Ford automobiles. But for some reason, Dad liked the car and kept it for the next 15 years. He soon traded in their other car, a nice Cutlass that had started to rust, for an almost identical Mercury, a year newer than the LTD.

I have had quite a few cars since then. Some were sporty and some were obvious Dad-mobiles. Although I liked some of them, I have never owned one that came close to measuring up to that lovely Pontiac.

23 Corvette Crazy

Steve Morrison

I joined the United States Air Force in 1968 after graduating from high school, and after being trained as a medic was stationed at the hospital in Wiesbaden, West Germany. When I arrived at the Frankfort airport, I could tell that I was in Germany because all I saw in the parking lots were Volkswagen Beetles! During the three and a half years I was stationed in Germany, I rarely saw an American automobile, let alone a real muscle car. One weekend a buddy and I decided to go to the races in Nurburg at the famous Nurburg race track. We hopped on a train and spent Friday night at a Bed and Breakfast hosted by an elderly German widow who served us one of the best breakfasts I have ever had. Then my buddy and I headed off to the races.

On that particular day there were eight t races, each one based on engine displacement. Most were smaller European cars and classes, but one of the races was classified as "open" which meant that anything with a motor and four wheels could be entered. When it came time for that race to start, my buddy and I were amazed to see a Corvette Stingray in the lineup. Whether it belonged to some American GI or a rich German I don't know, but it was definitely the hit of the race. When the start-your-engines call was announced, the other cars sounded like weed eaters while the 'Vette sounded like a rocket ship! Once the race started, the Corvette quickly left all of the other cars in the dust and soon began to lap them. The spectators were enthralled and were rooting with gusto for the Corvette to win. With one lap to go the Corvette blew its engine, but it still coasted across the finish line ahead of several of the other cars. Right then and there I decided that one way or another, someday I would own a Corvette.

When I was discharged from the Air Force, I returned to my parents' home and prepared to attend college using my GI Bill benefits. Since I planned to commute, I would need a vehicle, so I began to look for a Corvette. I had saved some money during my last year in the service, which would make a good down payment on my dream car. My dad and I combed through the local car lots and finally came across a 1966 Corvette convertible that was in my price range. After a test drive, I was sold and told the salesman that I would buy the car. My dad and I went to his insurance agent and made the arrangements. Needless to say, I was shocked at how much the insurance was going to cost, but it was too late—I had come down with a bad case of "Corvette Fever." As we were pulling into the dealership, I saw my Corvette driving away! The salesman had sold it to another guy while we were checking on insurance. I was not a happy camper and proceeded to tell the salesman where he could put his dealership!

Having no luck with dealerships I turned to "for sale" ads in the newspaper and finally found a 1967 Corvette Stingray Coupe. It was a 327 cubic-inch, 325 horsepower V-8 with a four-speed stick shift. It also had posi-traction and factory side pipes. It was mahogany brown with gold stripes and a black leather interior. In a word, it was beautiful. After a quick test drive, I bought it on the spot. The Corvette was incredibly fast! You did not pull out, you launched!

I soon learned that there were several perks to owning a Corvette. First, it was a status symbol of sorts, and second, there is a certain comradery among Corvette owners. We would smile and wave when we passed each other. I also discovered another perk on my first date with a local girl. When I kicked in the four-barrel on a back road, I could see her eyes shining with excitement and her breath coming quickly.

Of course, there were down sides too. My Corvette had a bad habit of getting stuck in second gear. If I did not want to drive home in second gear, I had to pull over and park, crawl under the car (which was no mean feat), and wearing a glove, move the linkage back and forth by hand until it loosened. This was a pain in dry weather and a real headache when it was raining! And then there was the fuel costs, the insurance costs, and the monthly car payment. After about a year and a half I decided that I and the Corvette would have to part company. I placed an ad in the newspaper but had little luck in finding a buyer. Finally, a fellow offered to take over the payments and trade me a 1968 Volkswagen Beetle. Sadly, I did the deal and with a flashback to my days in Germany, and finished my college career driving the Beetle. I had gone from the Penthouse to the outhouse! Even today when I see a Corvette, I get a little misty-eyed, remembering the beloved Brown Rocket of my college days.

24 The VW Campmobile

Michael Braswell

SINCE I WAS A boy growing up in a small-town farming community, I have always been partial to camping out. In those days, it didn't take much money to go to an Army-Navy surplus store and buy sleeping bag liners, canteens and other essentials. From being harassed by a horde of demonic sand fleas at St. George Island in my Boy Scout days to Bert, Charley and I being mistaken for Ku Klux Klan saboteurs near Tuskegee, Alabama, during a Christmas break, the camping life had its share of challenges. Still, the good times far outweigh the bad.

For a young married couple, camping remained a pleasurable, cost-effective vacation. In our recently purchased bright metallic-blue Opel Sportwagon with black leatherette seats and four-on-the-floor stick shift, we set out from southern Mississippi for a week-long jaunt west. Our first night was spent at Petit Jean State Park near Little Rock, Arkansas. It had a spectacular view and an excellent Lodge restaurant. Our destination for the second leg of our journey was Devil's Den State Park near Fayetteville. Perhaps a forewarning of the storm to come, when I pulled up behind an early 1950s Chevy on a rural paved road, I noted to my wife that something appeared to be odd about the car as it shimmied back and forth and sparks seemed to be flying up from the rear wheels. There looked to be five or six adults in the car, and even from a respectable distance behind it, I could hear country music blaring from the radio. Upon closer inspection, I realized the folks up ahead were, in fact, riding on the steel wheels. There were no tires on the wheels, just random strips of rubber flailing about. I quickly downshifted and passed them, imagining the sounds of "Dueling Banjos" emanating from their radio.

Arriving at Devil's Den, we checked in and set up our Sears and Roebuck army green umbrella tent. Since the park ranger told us a storm was expected in the evening, we ate an early supper and weatherproofed our tent as best we could. Then, the storm came. Amidst the rain, thunder, and lightning, we held on to the center tent pole for dear life to keep the tent from collapsing.

That's when I had the vision. Looking out at the raging storm battering the campground, I saw a VW Campmobile regally perched in its spot as though nothing was happening. I could see a fellow calmly reading a book at a well-lit table while the rest of us were clinging to what remained of our canvas abodes. I vowed then and there that one day I would own one of those majestic creatures. And two years later, I did.

I was teaching in Hattiesburg when I came across a 1969 VW Campmobile, not the Westfalia edition but plenty good enough for our needs and desires. Sixteen hundred dollars later, it was ours. Beige with an off-white pop-top, it stood proudly in our driveway. A sliding door, before sliding doors were cool, was located on the right side of the van. Inside it had a built-in water faucet and sink on top of a built-in cabinet that held an icebox in the bottom. Bucket seats up front and a bench seat in back that converted to what would barely pass as a full-size bed rounded out the basic interior amenities. Also included was a roll-out screened window on each side and a single full-size cot that could be attached when the pop-top was up. There was another canvas cot suitable for a small child that could be attached on top of the two front bucket seats. Our Campmobile had a four-speed stick shift and an AM radio up front to which I later added a cassette player. Our dream camper was powered by a mighty 40 horsepower air cooled engine located in the rear. I say "mighty" in jest. When ascending to the top of a hill, I would jam the accelerator to the floor, picking up as much speed as possible, which meant I would not have to downshift until halfway up the next hill.

Gary, who owned a regular VW van, and I would get together every month or so and tune up our vans. We would sit on our stools back-to-back and peruse my ring bound copy of "Volkswagen Maintenance for the Complete Idiot" before adjusting the timing and replacing spark plugs. A Styrofoam ice chest stocked with cold beverages kept us calm and cool.

In that era, there were a number of other young couples with growing families who went camping. State parks, private campgrounds, and beach camping were all popular with our caravan of chaos. The children ran wild until we corralled them, but when they were put to bed full of hotdogs and chips, it was "adult time" around the campfire.

We put a lot of miles on our Campmobile, sometimes with our young son and other times with just the two of us, when parents were babysitting. For several years we enjoyed our excursions, travelling from the Gulf to the mountains and through the Shenandoah Valley. While I'm not proud of it, I did experience a bit of perverse pleasure when we pulled into a campground in the midst of a downpour and popped our camper top, never having to step outside while other campers were scrambling to get their tents set up.

While visiting friends in Charlottesville, I received a call from East Tennessee State University offering me an interview for a teaching position. We spent the night before the interview at Rock Creek Park. It was one of the coldest nights ever recorded in the month of June. The long and short of it is that we accepted the offer and moved to the mountains, enjoying the next two years camping at Roan Mountain, traveling the Blue Ridge Parkway, and trying out other assorted camping opportunities. Then one day, a colleague asked me if I would be willing to part with our beloved Campmobile, and in a moment of weakness, I agreed to sell it to him. Now, all these many years and miles later, in the words of Johnny Cash, I still miss someone—our old VW Campmobile.

25 My Cars

Bill Carpenter

ONE THING THAT I have found interesting about my generation is our infatuation with the automobile. There has been a lot written about the automobile industry, especially the individuals who built it in the 1920s and '30s. I think we all are motivated for different reasons, but a common theme is obviously status, comfort, and the need for speed.

My parents didn't have a car until I was three or four years old, a very used 1938 Chevrolet coupe. In 1953, my dad bought our first new car, a Chevrolet 150 series two-door sedan. It was the most economical Chevrolet one could buy, a six-cylinder, three-speed on the column, basic car with fabric seats complete with a plastic covering that was never removed, and rubber floor covering. Seven years later, we traded for a 1960 Chevrolet Biscayne. Same song, second verse, a very basic car with the 235 six-cylinder and three-speed manual transmission. It had the same interior and no radio.

After that, things did improve, but I was understandably embarrassed by our car, as it reflected our status. At that time, there was a lot of societal emphasis on the car you owned. I regret feeling that way, but I'm confident that this experience has had a lot to do with the number and types of cars I have owned since then. To date, I have owned or built 29 vehicles. The most fun cars have been the five hard-top convertible Mercedes, three Corvettes, and three street rods. I have a lot of memories and learning experiences, both good and bad, with my hot rods.

In 1971, I was just out of the Army and convinced my wife we could afford an old pickup truck. I could use it to go to work and it would be useful for hauling stuff that our parents were giving us to start furnishing our home. My budget was limited to no more than $500, and I looked everywhere I could think of without much success. On a trip to Huntsville, Alabama, I found a 1953 Studebaker in Athens for $300, an all-stock farm truck with fresh red paint. Boy, was I an easy mark for that salesman! We almost made it to Huntsville before the truck began overheating and we had to stop at a local service station to put water in the radiator. The mechanic on duty said the real problem was that the battery was reversed, and that should have been a hint we were in the wrong place. I later learned that Fords and Studebakers of that era ran on reverse polarity. In any event, the next weekend we went to pick up the truck and make our way back to Nashville. On the way home, I was on I- 65, with my wife following, when a Tennessee State Trooper lit me up. I had no idea what was going on because I knew there was no way the truck could exceed the speed limit. The officer asked how much I had been drinking that day. Normally at that time in my life, I might have been drinking or had a six pack in the truck, but not on that day. My wife pulled up behind the trooper and was walking up to see what was going on when the officer quickly advised her to return to her vehicle. He informed me that I was weaving and not staying within my lane of traffic. The reason, I explained, was that the front end was so worn out that there was a lot of play in the steering wheel, and I had to constantly move the truck from left to right to stay in a straight line. I guess he felt sorry for me because he laughed and told me to go straight home, and not drive on the Interstate in the future.

In the late 1980s, I decided to build my first street rod. I have always loved classic pickups and found a 1957 step-side, stock five-window truck. It took over three years to complete the job, but the finished product was a Midnight Blue paint scheme with a stock 350 chevy small-block engine and a turbo transmission. To this day, I regret selling that truck more than any of my others. During the time I owned it, I spent many hours learning about body work and restoration.

My favorite memory of the '57 happened when we had completed almost all of the work. I was dying to take it out and see how it felt to drive it. We didn't have the accelerator cable hooked up to the carburetor or a seat in the car, so my mechanic friend said he could run a cable from the carburetor through a hole in the dash and I could sit on a milk crate we had in the shop. Sounded good to me. In front of the shop was a long straightaway and very little traffic (thank goodness). Perhaps you can visualize this, but I pulled on the cable hard without knowing how much resistance there would be on the throttle, and the g-force was so strong I fell off of the milk crate and had to hang on to the steering wheel for dear life. After I regained my balance and I could look back through the tire smoke, I could see everyone bent over with laughter.

After running with my car friends for several years, the peer pressure to be a member of the group with a pre-48 vehicle and to be accepted as a member of the NSRA was too much for me, so I decided to buy or build a pre-48 hot rod. I sold my '57 and started my quest to find the right car. I remembered that my high school friend had a '39 Chevrolet Coupe his father had built for him while he was in the Navy. I had always thought it was a really cool car and wanted to see if he still had it. I called and, yes, he still had the car but he wasn't ready to sell it. I asked him to call me if he ever changed his mind. About a year later he called me back and I was able to purchase my dream hot rod project car.

My friend's father had built a very reliable car, and he had used the car to commute to Middle Tennessee State University while he was completing his college education. His father had replaced the rear end with a '57 Chevy truck rear suspension. The power train was from a late '60s small journal 327 combined with a Muncie four-speed transmission. The Candy Apple Red paint was pretty faded, but it still had all of the original chrome. The interior was black with front seats from a late '60s Volkswagen and jump seats in the back.

I still remember going to Watertown to pick up the car. My friend's parents watched as we loaded the car on my trailer. I'm sure it was a little sad for them to see the car go to a new home, but I think they knew it was going to be well taken care of. Like most guys, I had a pretty good idea what I wanted to do with the car, and I had talked many times about my plans with my mechanic-car-builder buddy. We replaced the front end with an aftermarket Mustang II suspension and disc brakes. The brake system was further upgraded with a Corvette master cylinder mounted under the car instead of on the firewall. The engine was sent to a performance shop for a thorough cleaning and, while there, was bored 30 over with the heads milled to 2.02. When we got it back, it was installed with high compression pistons, new rods, valves, and a 280 cam. The intake was changed several times, but the last one installed was an Edelbrock high rise with an Edelbrock 650 CFM carburetor. I also changed the four-speed transmission to a Tremec six-speed out of a wrecked Camaro. The paint scheme was Indigo Blue with a splash of orange.

There are always stories that go along with a car build and ownership, but one of my favorites happened one Sunday afternoon after my mechanic and I had gone through the car, checking the carburetor and timing for an upcoming trip to a car show in Evansville, Indiana. We were going to Murfreesboro to grab some lunch and were basically running the car a little extra hard to make sure everything checked out. He was driving, and we had just stopped at a red light, when this guy pulls up beside us in a Mustang 5.0, revving his engine. The mechanic never looked at the guy, but looked over at me knowing I was anxious to see how the '39 would run. I have known a lot of guys who were good street racers, but this fellow was one of the best going through the gears. We beat the Mustang to the next light by about a car length. When the guy pulled up beside us, I could tell he was embarrassed and a little mad at himself for getting beat by an old Chevy. He wanted to run again to show us that the last time was a fluke. This time the accelerator never left the floor through all four gears. It wasn't even close. There is something cool and joyous about two

50-plus-year-olds drag racing like a couple teenagers. I have since sold that car to my mechanic. It was the right thing to do because he had put so much time and skill into building it into a great car, while teaching me a lot about the restoration and building of a high-performance engine.

My current passion is a '28 Ford Model AA pickup. It was partially built when I bought it, but the owner had lost interest in completing the build. I bought the car thinking I would be happy with it as it was, but it seems I always want something a little different. With the help of my friends, we have basically rebuilt the car. It might say *Ford* on the outside, but it's all Chevrolet underneath with a Corvette suspension and powered by a small block Chevrolet engine. The engine was a stock 350, but I have replaced it with a 1969 Corvette 327. It has been built similar to the '39's 327, but not quite as radical. It's fast enough for a soon-to-be 73-year-old Boomer.

The great thing about cars is that everyone can have one that gives them pleasure. I love the '50s, '60s and early '70s cars. We were blessed to have been born in this generation because things will never be the same for us when these cars are finally gone from the road.

26 God's Four Plus One

George Spain

INSIDE MY HEAD I was grown, but everything else about me was sixteen.

It's well known to those of us who are advanced in years and wiser than most of humanity, that a 1953 powder-blue Cadillac Coupe de Ville Convertible with tail-fins, a white canvas top, gleaming spoke whitewall tires, and white leather upholstery, was made in Heaven by you know WHO. My father had one on his car lot, GEORGE SPAIN MOTOR COMPANY, and "Lord have mercy", he let me drive it the night of our Senior Graduation Banquet.

"The Cadillac Man", as my father was known by his many customers: politicians, police officials, heads of numbers rackets, preachers of every "True Church," any and every sort of humanity that had the money to buy his cars, loved me because of that, and showed it.

Dressed in black tuxedos, black bow ties, stiff-white shirts, and shiny black shoes, my friends and I were five knights-errant seeking adventure and glory. Every stich on us was rented from "Sam Bittner's Formal Wear & Costumes".

We had graduated three hours before at David Lipscomb High School, a private Church of Christ school. After stuffing ourselves at the banquet and quickly rushing our dates home, we were free at last. It was time for our reward – on a balmy summer night, we were cruising in the most beautiful car in Nashville. Could heaven be any better than this?

Who knows, the Lord may have been guiding us, for we turned up 5th from Broad and "Yea Verily Behold!", there was a mass of people going into the Grand Old Opry House. Above the entrance inscribed on a large banner was "WALLY FOWLER'S ALL NIGHT GOSPEL SINGING."

I slowed as we passed by. There was an alley beside the Ryman with a well-lit side door that read "Performer's Entrance". Immediately we all pointed to it as and shouted together, "Let's sneak in!"

Within the five minutes it took to round the block, we had worked out a plan. Coupled with our matching tuxedos, honest smiling faces and our piece de resistance, the powder-blue 1953 Cadillac Coupe de Ville Convertible with tail-fins, white canvas top, gleaming spoke whitewall tires, and white leather upholstery, would surely be enough to get by a Nashville policeman.

After telling the others to keep their mouths shut, smile, and let me do the talking, I pulled into the alley and stopped as the policeman approached. He held his hat in his left-hand while wiping sweat from his well-fed, flushed face. He was looking at the car, not us. When he approached the front of the Cadillac, he stuffed his handkerchief into his pocket, and ran his hand over the smooth curve of the left front fender, smiling as though . . . well as though it was . . . you know.

I stepped out of the car, "Officer."

He looked up with a smile, "Yes Suh, what can I do ta hep?"

Sir, we're the "God's Four Plus One", and are supposed to perform in thirty minutes. Can we leave our car here?"

"Sure boys, leave tha keys with me an I'll watch her like she wus my own."

We all thanked him as he held the performer's door open for us to file in. A few strides later, we found ourselves in the dressing room area. People were everywhere, their movements, the lights, smells, and sounds were befuddling. We pushed on toward a beautiful sound of "Onward Christian Soldiers."

Suddenly, we found ourselves at the edge of the stage, hidden by the curtains. We watched for a bit, then eased across the corner of the stage, down a few steps, and sat in some empty seats on the front row.

We stayed there long enough to complete our performance, then went back up the steps, through the dressing rooms, and out the door into the alley. God love that good officer, he was beaming like an angel as he opened the Cadillac's door, "Well boys how'd it go?"

"Super, Sir. Thanks for watching our car." I gave him a $5 tip and we drove away into that glorious night, leaving a memory that remains with me even now, 68 years later.

There is a profound lesson in this true story. It is this –

PARENTS, NEVER LET YOUR CHILDREN DRIVE YOUR BEST CAR ON GRADUATION NIGHT!